THE EUCHARISTIC PRAYER
OF ADDAI AND MARI

THE
EUCHARISTIC PRAYER
OF
ADDAI AND MARI

A. Gelston

CLARENDON PRESS · OXFORD
1992

Oxford University Press, Walton Street, Oxford OX2 6DP
Oxford New York Toronto
Delhi Bombay Calcutta Madras Karachi
Petaling Jaya Singapore Hong Kong Tokyo
Nairobi Dar es Salaam Cape Town
Melbourne Auckland
and associated companies in
Berlin Ibadan

Oxford is a trade mark of Oxford University Press

Published in the United States
by Oxford University Press, New York

British Library Cataloguing in Publication Data
Gelston, Anthony 1935–
The eucharistic prayer of Addai and Mari.
1. Christian church. Eucharist. Eucharistic prayers
I. Title
264.36
ISBN 0-19-826737-1

Library of Congress Cataloguing in Publication Data
The Eucharistic prayer of Addai and Mari | A. Gelston
Text of prayer in Syriac with commentary in English.
Includes bibliographical references and index.
1. Eucharistic prayers. 2. Lord's Supper (Liturgy)—Texts.
3. Syriac Church—Liturgy—Texts. 4. Eucharistic prayers—History
and criticism. 5. Lord's Supper (Liturgy)—Texts—History and
criticism. 6. Syrian Church—Liturgy—Texts—History and criticism.
I. Title.
BX177.A2 1991 264'.015—dc20 90-46435
ISBN 0-19-826737-1

Set by Imprint, Oxford
At Oxford University Computing Service
Printed in Great Britain by
Bookcraft (Bath) Ltd., Midsomer Norton, Avon

To Archdeacon Yonan and the British
Congregation of the Assyrian Church of the East,
who use this Eucharistic Prayer in their Liturgy

PREFACE

The original form of the *Anaphora of the Apostles* has been the object of great speculation, and justly so. It is clearly one of the most ancient eucharistic prayers still in use today; it was, or at least became, the principal anaphora of those Syriac-using churches that were least influenced by the Hellenistic culture of the Roman Empire; and it can be considered a representative expression of the Judeo-Christianity of the early centuries of the Christian era. The time and place of its first composition are shrouded in the mists of time.

(W. F. Macomber, 1982)

SPARSITY of evidence is a soil in which speculation can easily become rampant. The most serious obstacle confronting the modern student of this ancient Eucharistic Prayer is the lack as yet of any MS text earlier than the tenth century. On the other hand, the evident relationship between much of this anaphora and the Maronite anaphora commonly known (from its opening word) as *Sharar*, which has been recognized since Rahmani (1899) and Baumstark (1904), opens up the possibility of a critical examination of this relationship which can take us some way in our quest for the original form of the Anaphora of Addai and Mari.

The time is clearly not ripe to attempt a definitive study of this anaphora from the point of view of either textual or literary criticism. It has been thought useful, however, as a contribution to the continuing debate, to attempt to prepare a working critical text, on eclectic principles, of the medieval anaphora of the oldest extant MSS. Macomber (1966) put all students in his debt by publishing 'the oldest known text of the Anaphora of the Apostles Addai and Mari' viz. that contained in the Ḥudra belonging to the Church of Mar Esh'aya in Mosul. Together with this text he published a list of fifty-two other known MSS, a critical apparatus recording their readings where they differ from the Mar Esh'aya text, and notes on some of the variant readings. Webb (1967–8) published a list of MSS of this anaphora at the end of an article in which he considered divergent readings in the text of the eucharistic rite as a whole, the greater number of which occur in the pre-anaphoral part of the liturgy. Spinks (1980) published an English translation of Macomber's text and apparatus, enriched by variants from a dozen MSS that had not been used by Macomber. These were contributed by Webb, who also supplied an introductory note to the MSS. Despite the immense value of the material published by Macomber, Webb, and Spinks, there remains a need for a critical hand-text of the anaphora. Macomber's text is essentially a diplomatic reproduction of the Mar Esh'aya text, and as such suffers from three disadvantages for the ordinary student. A few idiosyncratic, and even erroneous, readings of this MS are given unnecessary prominence. Text-critical judgements appear only in the notes. The Ḥudra follows the common practice of abbreviating Qanona forms and congregational responses, and this makes it difficult to read the text as a continuous whole. The principles on which the working critical text offered here was prepared are explained in the immediate introduction to the Text. The only additional point to be made here is that the needs of the liturgical student with little or no Syriac have been constantly borne in mind. It is indeed hoped that this may prove a useful text for relative beginners in Syriac.

At this point mention must be made of the Webb Archive. The late Douglas Webb collected a substantial number of transcripts of the MS texts of this anaphora and of other East Syrian liturgical texts. These transcripts were made in his own very clear hand, and where it has been possible to check his transcripts against the originals or microfilms or photocopies of the originals, the transcripts have proved to evince a very high degree of accuracy. It is a matter of profound regret that Webb did not live to publish a critical apparatus of the variants contained in these transcripts. Full use, however, has been made of them in the preparation of the edition. It is hoped that the ordinary student will find the text offered here a useful basis for study, and that even the student with no Syriac will be able to some extent to form his or her own judgement on questions of textual criticism with the help of the textual notes that follow it.

The other area of study in which it is possible to hope for some degree of objectivity is the critical examination of the relationship between the Anaphora of Addai and Mari and *Sharar*. The publication of a critical text of the latter by Sauget (1973) has made possible a more scientific evaluation of the relationship between the two anaphoras than was open to Engberding, whose pioneering work (1932, 1957) in this sphere, however, remains of great value. Macomber (1982) was the first to attempt a detailed comparison of the two anaphoras since the publication of Sauget's text of *Sharar* (generally known thus from its opening word 'Confirm'). The fact that reason has been found at several points to evaluate the evidence differently from Macomber, particularly at those points where the texts of the two anaphoras diverge sharply, indicates that no final results can yet be expected in this area of study. For a significant part of the anaphora, however, it is possible to attain assured results within reasonably narrow limits, and this does mean that for this part of the text we can penetrate behind the medieval MS tradition to something much closer to the state of the text at the beginning of the fifth century. In the interests of objectivity this part of the study has been confined to the Commentary and to the conjectural reconstruction offered in the Appendix.

Attention has also been paid in the Introduction and Commentary to parallels with other eucharistic texts. It may be useful here to point out that little reference has been made to the prayers in *Didache* 9–10, because it is by no means certain that they are eucharistic, and none to the Strasbourg Papyrus, because of uncertainties about its date and its completeness.

The twentieth century has witnessed the growth of a widespread interest in the Anaphora of Addai and Mari. The greatest contributions have been made by Engberding, Macomber, Spinks, and Webb, and where I have ventured to disagree with them I have done so with the greatest respect, and with a profound awareness of my indebtedness to their industry and their insights. The range of speculation generated by this anaphora and the scope afforded to it by the relative sparsity of objective evidence are cause for some anxiety. I have attempted in the present work to make a contribution to the continuing discussion which is constrained as far as possible by objective evidence. It is my hope that this will serve to clarify the discussion to some extent, if only by indicating that some lines of argument are unlikely to lead to assured results. Where appropriate, I have offered comments on the work of those who have written before me, but this has usually been necessary for the elucidation of particular points. I have made no attempt to comment on everything that has been written; to do so would require a substantial study in its own right. Many of the speculative positions that have been put forward are of a kind that can be neither proved nor disproved in the present state of the evidence, and they often depend in turn on positions adopted in relation to other controverted areas. Some of these issues are addressed briefly in the Introduction and in the introduction to the Commentary, but no claim is made to comprehensiveness. Some significant older contributions are simply listed in the Bibliography.

In any case fresh studies continue to appear. All the work on the Text and practically the whole of that on the Commentary was done during six months of research leave in 1987. Regrettably the studies of Magne (1987) and Marston (1989) came to my attention too late to be taken into consideration during the preparation of the Commentary. This is particularly unfortunate in the case of Magne's study because, like the present work, it attempts a reconstruction of the common core of the Anaphora of Addai and Mari and *Sharar*. It goes further in an attempt to trace the oldest components of this core to two separate hymns addressed to Christ, and only secondarily adapted for use as a Eucharistic Prayer. This study requires a far more thorough evaluation than is possible at this stage in the present work, but an initial reading leaves the impression that much of the analysis is speculative. Magne's argument for the antiquity of 1.51, for instance, fails to take into account the absence of the word ܒܫܡܟ ('in thy name') in the two oldest MSS. Marston in turn offers no evidence for the excisions he proposes, and his assumption that the anaphora was originally a thanksgiving for the Lord's Prayer seems arbitrary.

The present work was at an advanced stage of preparation when I had the opportunity to see B. D. Spinks's thesis: 'With Angels and Archangels: The Background, Form and Function of the Sanctus in the Eucharistic Prayer' (1988), which is about to be published under the title 'The Sanctus in the Eucharistic Prayer' (CUP). The thesis inevitably touches on the same ground as parts of the present work, and at certain points reaches different conclusions, but I have not felt it necessary to rewrite what I had already completed independently in order to take note of points on which I differ from Spinks. I am, however, indebted to the thesis for reminding me of a detail in Macomber (1966), which I had overlooked.

Pressure of other work prevented me from completing this edition until the summer of 1989. I am very conscious of the speed with which some areas of discussion are moving on, and of considerable areas of research that still need to be carried out. I offer this study in the hope that it will be a useful contribution to the continuing discussion, and ask only that my own modest speculations be evaluated in the light of such evidence as is or will become available.

A. G.

Durham
30 September 1989

ACKNOWLEDGEMENTS

I WISH to record my gratitude to the authorities of the British Library, the Cambridge University Library, the Bodleian Library, Oxford, the Central Library, Selly Oak Colleges, Birmingham, and the John Rylands University Library of Manchester for allowing me to consult MSS in their possession. I also wish to thank the Staatsbibliothek Preussischer Kulturbesitz, Berlin, Orientabteilung, for supplying me with microfilms of the MSS Sachau 354 and Assfalg 29, and to Professor H. P. Rüger and Dr M. Kellermann for help in locating these MSS. Dr P. B. Dirksen, Director of the Peshiṭta Institute in the University of Leiden, kindly procured me a microfilm of the MS Leiden Or. 1215, and the Revd Professor W. D. McHardy very kindly allowed me to work on the McHardy Codex at his home. Dr S. P. Brock of the Oriental Institute, University of Oxford, arranged for me to spend a week in the Institute working on the transcripts in the Webb Archive, and allowed me to borrow a few of the microfilms from the archive. He also kindly verified a reading for me, and supplied me with numerous bibliographical details. The Revd B. Mastin kindly verified several readings for me at the Cambridge University Library. The Central Staff Research Fund of the University of Durham gave me a grant to cover the cost of travel to Birmingham, Cambridge, Cullen, London, Manchester, and Oxford to examine MSS.

I also wish to thank Dr W. F. Macomber for the gift of photocopies of his transcripts of the Mar Esh'aya text of the Anaphoras of Theodore and Nestorius, and for considerable help in identifying some of the MSS listed by himself and the late Revd Douglas Webb, as well as for information about some of the MSS. The late Revd Dr G. J. Cuming kindly gave me his set of photocopies and offprints of articles on the Anaphora of Addai and Mari. The Revd Dr B. D. Spinks has presented me with offprints of his own publications, and has also provided several useful pieces of information. The Revd Dr J. Fenwick provided a useful bibliographical reference. Señora

P. M. Morán supplied me with an English translation of the article of J. M. Sánchez Caro. The staff of the Inter-Library Loan service in the University Library at Durham have given me considerable help in procuring much of the secondary literature required for this study.

I also wish to thank the authorities of Cambridge University Press for permission to use material from my article 'Sacrifice in the early East Syrian Eucharistic Tradition' in the volume of essays entitled *Sacrifice and Redemption*, edited by S. W. Sykes. The substance of the Commentary of Sections E–F was read as a paper to the Society for Liturgical Study on 1 September 1988.

The Revd Professor James Barr kindly introduced this work to the Delegates of the Oxford University Press, and I am most grateful to the Delegates for accepting it for the publication, and to the staff of the Press for much practical help and advice. I am grateful too to Mrs Catherine Griffin of Imprint for overcoming the problems of setting a complicated manuscript in type.

Generous subventions towards the cost of publication were made by the Hall-Houghton Trustees and the Publications Board of the University of Durham, and these are gratefully acknowledged.

My greatest debt is to my wife for her constant encouragement, for reading the typescript at every stage of the preparation of this work, and for practical help in checking both the typescript and the proofs.

I had been unable before this work went to press to obtain or see the edition of the Anaphora of Theodore by J. Vadakkel: *The East Syrian Anaphora of Mar Theodore of Mopsuestia* (Oriental Institute of Religious Studies Publications 129, Kottayam, 1989).

I wish finally to acknowledge the help and stimulus I have received from the publications of other scholars. My indebtedness to them is apparent on every page, and I have tried to include in the bibliography all the works on which I have drawn. I apologize if I have omitted any by inadvertence.

CONTENTS

ABBREVIATIONS

ATR	*Anglican Theological Review*
CSCO	Corpus Scriptorum Christianorum Orientalium
EL	*Ephemerides Liturgicae*
JEH	*Journal of Ecclesiastical History*
JJS	*Journal of Jewish Studies*
JLW	*Jahrbuch für Liturgiewissenschaft*
JQR	*Jewish Quarterly Review*
JTS	*Journal of Theological Studies*
LEW	*see* Bibliography s.v. Brightman
LMD	*La Maison-Dieu*
OC	*Oriens Christianus*
OCA	Orientalia Christiana Analecta
OCP	*Orientalia Christiana Periodica*
OS	*L'Orient syrien*
PG	J.-P. Migne, *Patrologia Graeca*
PdO	*Parole de l'Orient*
PO	Patrologia Orientalis
QL	*Questions liturgiques*
PEER	*see* Bibliography s.v. Jasper and Cuming
RHE	*Revue d'histoire ecclésiastique*
SC	Sources Chrétiennes
SE	*Sacris Erudiri*
SL	*Studia Liturgica*
SP	*Studia Patristica*
TB	Babylonian Talmud
TS	*Theological Studies*
TU	Texte und Untersuchungen
VC	*Vigiliae Christianae*

INTRODUCTION

THE present work contains a critical edition of the medieval text of the Eucharistic Prayer or Anaphora of Addai and Mari, together with a literary and historical commentary which attempts to determine the oldest elements in it. The original nucleus, if it could be precisely determined, would be a document of the first importance for the history of the Eucharistic Prayer in early Christian worship. Even in its earliest attainable form it is an extremely significant text. The purpose of this Introduction is to set it in its wider context.

In the first section we shall examine the relationship between Jewish liturgical forms and the early development of the Christian Eucharistic Prayer with reference to the Last Supper, which is the immediate origin of that prayer. In the second section we shall examine the evidence for the emergence of fixed forms in early Christian eucharistic practice. Both of these are large and important areas of research in their own right, and no attempt will be made to give even a complete account of the 'state of the question'. Nor will any attempt be made to comment on all the studies that have included a discussion of the Anaphora of Addai and Mari. Some specific theories will, however, be subjected to critical review, and it will be shown that the evidence hardly warrants some of the conclusions that have been based on it. What will emerge clearly is indeed the relative paucity of precise early evidence, which should make us beware of too facile attempts to trace a direct linear evolution from specific Jewish forms to the Anaphora of Addai and Mari. The third section provides an outline of the origins of the East Syrian Church, a brief summary of what is known of the Eucharistic Prayer in the East Syrian tradition, and a brief consideration of the relation of this to the Syrian tradition as a whole.

A. From the Last Supper to the Eucharist

The almost universal presence in the Eucharistic Prayer of an Institution Narrative linking the Eucharist to the Last Supper is a natural starting-point for an investigation into the evolution and significance of this prayer, of which that of Addai and Mari is one of the earliest extant examples. Christians have generally celebrated the Eucharist in obedience to the dominical command to 'Do this in remembrance of me' (1 Cor. 11: 24). At the Last Supper Jesus gave thanks over the bread and cup, although none of the New Testament narratives gives any indication of the content of his thanksgiving. The Eucharistic Prayer is the direct counterpart in the Christian liturgy of Jesus' thanksgiving at the Last Supper. During the present century liturgical scholars have taken seriously the fact that Jesus and his original disciples were Jews, and that the Last Supper was therefore a Jewish religious meal. Much time and effort have been devoted to the study of Jewish liturgical forms in the hope that these will yield some indication of the likely content of Jesus' own thanksgiving and also of that of the Eucharistic prayers of the first Christians.

This whole area of research is, however, beset by a number of difficulties. In the first place the occasion, and therefore the precise nature, of the Last Supper itself remains a matter of dispute. While the Synoptic Gospels clearly identify it with the Passover meal, the chronology of the Fourth Gospel equally clearly indicates that the Passover meal was due to be eaten on the evening of Good Friday after Jesus' death. New Testament scholarship remains divided over whether the Last Supper was the Passover meal or not, and if not, what kind of a religious meal it was. It is not possible to enter this discussion here, but the importance of the question can readily be recognized from the theoretical possibility that, were the Last Supper to be demonstrably identified as the Passover meal, the study of the Passover liturgy itself might give a fair indication of the likely content of the thanksgiving offered by Jesus at the Supper.

It is certainly possible to draw a broad picture of Palestinian Jewish religious practice at the time of Jesus, in which the three focal points were the Temple in Jerusalem, the local synagogue, and the home. The last two were the ones that figured most in the life of the ordinary Jew, and if he did not live in or near Jerusalem, pilgrimages to the Temple were only occasional experiences. Sacrifice was restricted to the Temple, but the Passover meal, which was held in the home or a temporary substitute for it, was closely related to sacrifice in that the Passover lamb had first been offered as a sacrifice in the Temple. The main outline of the religious calendar, punctuated by the weekly Sabbath and the monthly New Moon as well as by the great annual festivals of Passover, Weeks, and Tabernacles, not to mention more recent festivals such as that of the Dedication mentioned in John 10: 22, is also clear. One might therefore expect to gain some inkling of the content of Jesus' thanksgivings at the Last Supper from a study of the Passover liturgy.

Such an expectation seems, however, likely to be largely disappointed. For a second area of difficulty concerns the date and nature of the early evidence for Jewish liturgical practice. Apart from Old Testament passages that were used in Jewish worship, most of the earliest evidence for the liturgical practices of at any rate Rabbinical Judaism is that contained in the *Mishnah*. Although many of the contents of this collection are much earlier, it did not reach its definitive form until the end of the second century AD. It is not easy to demonstrate that a particular practice was already observed in the time of Jesus' ministry. In general the only criteria for dating specific traditions are references to Temple practice, which antedate the destruction of the Temple in AD 70, or sayings attributed to named rabbis whose dates are known. Even so, the handling of material that had long been transmitted orally requires careful discrimination, with the result that while the broad outlines of practice are reasonably clear, very little precise detail can be established with certainty for the period of Christian origins. Even in Talmudic times the writing down of prayers was forbidden (TB *Shabbath* 115b), and there is much reason to question the extent to which fixed non-scriptural forms existed in the early part of the first century AD.

At first sight the mention of some of the benedictions by name in the *Mishnah*, e.g. those of the *Tephillah* on New Year's Day (*Rosh ha-Shanah* 4. 5, Danby, 1933, p.193; cf. also *Tamid* 5. 1, *ibid.*, p.586), suggests that they had already attained a fixed form, but this would be a misleading inference. Heinemann (1977) has drawn attention to the existence of multiple versions of prayers in early times followed later by a tendency towards standardization: 'Only the number of the benedictions, their order of recitation, and their general content

had been fixed, as well as the occasions of their recitation and the
rules which governed them, but not their exact wording' (p. 26).
Berakoth 4. 3–4 (Danby, p. 5) indicates that either the *Eighteen
Benedictions* or the 'substance' of the *Eighteen* could be prayed, and
records a dictum of Rabbi Eliezer (*c.* AD 100) warning against
making a prayer a 'fixed task' (whether the word denotes precisely
a fixed formula is not clear). A similar dictum is ascribed to a
contemporary of Eliezer in *Aboth* 2. 13 (Danby, p. 449). Further
indications that the precise wording of the benedictions was not fixed
are to be found in TB *Berakoth*. In 34a the contrast is recorded
between two of Eliezer's disciples who prayed the *Tephillah*, the one
at great length and the other with great brevity. In 48b–49a the need
to mention certain items in particular benedictions is recorded, while
in 29b it is urged that something new be said in the recitation of the
Tephillah. This evidence indicates clearly that the precise content of
even so central a prayer as the *Tephillah* (or *Eighteen Benedictions*) was
far from attaining a fixed form by the beginning of the second
century. There can therefore be no appeal to a liturgical formula
which Jesus may be presumed to have used at the Last Supper. Reif
(1983), in a survey of Jewish liturgical research, goes so far as to say
(p. 168): 'Suddenly it becomes clear that the basic work in Jewish
liturgy has, after all, not been definitively completed. *Au contraire*,
even the most basic facts about the early liturgical relationship
between Jews and Christians must be rethought.'

A further telling observation of Heinemann (1977, ch. 7) is that
the Lord's Prayer belongs, from a form-critical point of view, to the
category of private and non-statutory prayer, a distinction reinforced
by the context as given in Matt. 6: 5–6. The prayer of Jesus in
Gethsemane also belongs to this category, while the opening of Jesus'
prayer in Matt. 11: 25–6 'I thank thee' is also characteristic of private
prayer. Such prayers enjoyed an even greater freedom of expression
than the statutory prayers, and Bouley (1981, p. 47) even suggests
that the recognition at the supper table at Emmaus was occasioned
by a distinctive meal-blessing used by Jesus. This factor further
reduces the possibility of reconstructing the content of Jesus' thanksgiving at the Last Supper from later Jewish sources.

The last of these examples reminds us that the opening 'I thank
thee' is characteristic of the Qumran hymns. It needs to be remembered that Palestinian Judaism in the time of Jesus was by no means
uniform. The controversy over the Qumran community and its

relation to other known sects or parties in Judaism at the turn of the era indicates both that there were several other forms of Judaism than the Pharisaic, which was to give rise to the Rabbinic Judaism of the period after the destruction of the Temple in AD 70, and that our knowledge of the practices of these other sects is very limited. The fact that the alternative ritual calendar of Qumran has been invoked in the exploration of the relationship of the Last Supper to the Passover indicates the possibility that the Jewish religious practice of Jesus and his disciples was not Pharisaic at all. We have then to admit that the quest for the content of Jesus' thanksgiving at the Last Supper among Jewish liturgical forms has so far proved unsuccessful and is likely to remain so. At most we can claim that Jesus belonged to a religious tradition to which later accessible Jewish liturgical forms also belonged, and that we can discern from the latter something of the probable general atmosphere of the Last Supper.

In the next section we shall take note of the not inconsiderable evidence that the wording of the Christian Eucharistic prayer remained far from fixed until at least the beginning of the third century. There is no hint of a tradition that the actual content of Jesus' thanksgiving at the Last Supper was remembered, transmitted, and repeated at the celebration of the Eucharist. What was done in remembrance of Jesus was the offering of thanks, but not according to a fixed formula. The Jewish origins of the first Christians, however, make it likely that the early Eucharistic Prayers were influenced by Jewish usage and, surprising as it may seem, there is evidence for the continuing influence of Jewish worship on Christian as late as the fourth century (Fiensy, 1985, pp. 5, 215–19; he mentions particularly Chrysostom's need to preach to the Christians in Antioch *c.* AD 386 to dissuade them from being lured to the worship in the synagogue). If Syrian Christianity preserved links with Judaism and continued Jewish practices longer than most Christians, it may still be reasonable to look for traces of a direct formative influence of later Jewish liturgical practice on developing Christian practice. This may prove to be more significant than the origin of the Eucharist in the Last Supper.

Before we explore this further, however, there are yet other areas of uncertainty to be noted. The most important ones are the relation of the Eucharist to the Agape and the emergence of the Lord's Day as the regular occasion for the celebration of the Eucharist in the primitive Church. While the evidence required to trace these developments in detail is simply not available, there can be no doubt that both of them influenced the form and content of the eucharistic thanksgiving. One obvious point is the combination of the originally separate benedictions over the bread and the cup into a single Eucharistic Prayer. The uncertainty whether the prayers in *Didache* 9–10 are to be referred to the Eucharist or to an Agape already distinct from it further complicates these questions, and it is not appropriate to explore them further in the present context.

The areas of Jewish liturgical practice where we might expect to find the most direct influence on the development of the early Christian Eucharistic Prayer are the meal-blessings in general and the usages of the Passover meal in particular. For the former we may turn in the first place to *Berakoth* 7. 3 (Danby, p. 8), where one of the formulae for introducing the meal-blessing is: 'We will bless the Lord our God', or, as it might equally well be translated, 'Let us bless the Lord our God'. This has an obvious affinity with the formula attested already in the introductory dialogue of the Eucharistic Prayer in the *Apostolic Tradition* of Hippolytus: *Gratias agamus Domino*. Heinemann (1962) comes to the interesting conclusion that the formulae in this *Mishnah* are early and preserved specific characteristics of early *ḥavurah* tradition as against common form-patterns adopted as standard for synagogue prayers in later times. It is quite possible therefore that this widespread formula does represent continuity with one remembered detail of what was said at the Last Supper, even though it comes in the introduction to the thanksgiving rather than the thanksgiving itself. At least this formula suggests that the meal-blessing is a more likely source for the Christian Eucharistic Prayer than the benedictions *Yoṣer* and *Ahabah* preceding the recitation of the *Shemaʿ* in the morning service (on which see the introduction to the Commentary).

As for the Passover meal, some details are to be found in *Pesahim* 10. 1–7 (Danby, pp. 150–1). The information to be gleaned from this passage for the liturgical content of this observance contains little in the way of verbal formulas, although 10. 5 contains a formula for the introduction of the Hallel Psalms (113–18) after the recitation of the Passover Haggadah in which the father explains to his son the significance of the several distinctive features of the meal in relation to the events of the Exodus which it commemorates. This passage is quoted in the Commentary on Section D of the Anaphora of Addai and Mari, and it affords suggestive, though not precise, parallels to early Christian material as indicated there.

The quest for actual Jewish forms of thanksgiving that may have provided the origins of the Christian Eucharistic Prayer has generally centred on the *Birkath ha-mazon*, the thanksgiving at the end of the meal. The oldest text of this is that of the tenth-century Siddur Rav Saadya Gaon. In this text the thanksgiving falls into four sections, at the end of the third of which a long insertion is made at Passover just before the final benediction. This embolism refers repeatedly to the theme of remembrance, which has suggested a possible connection with Jesus' instruction to 'do this' in remembrance of him. Finkelstein (1928–9, pp. 217–8) establishes on the basis of *Berakoth* 6. 8 and TB *Berakoth* 48b that the fourth of these benedictions was added at the earliest after the fall of Jerusalem in AD 70. So it is reasonable to suppose that the essence of the first three benedictions was in use in the time of Jesus, even though the content will still have been fluid. This then is the text most likely to have influenced early Christian practice.

The text of the first three benedictions, without embolisms, reads:

Blessed are you, Lord our God, King of the universe, for you nourish us and the whole world with goodness, grace, kindness, and mercy.
Blessed are you, Lord, for you nourish the universe.

We will give thanks to you, Lord our God, because you have given us for our inheritance a desirable land, good and wide, the covenant and the law, life and food.
And for all these things we give you thanks and bless your name for ever and beyond.
Blessed are you, Lord, for the land and for food.

Have mercy, Lord our God, on us your people Israel, and your city Jerusalem, on your sanctuary and your dwelling place, on Zion, the habitation of your glory, and the great and holy house over which your name is invoked. Restore the kingdom of the house of David to its place in our days, and speedily build Jerusalem.
Blessed are you, Lord, for you build Jerusalem. Amen. (*PEER*, pp. 10–11)

It may be observed that the three benedictions are different in both form and content. The first is a benediction in the strict sense (beginning 'Blessed are you'), and is essentially a thanksgiving for food. The second is formally a thanksgiving, and its primary concern is to give thanks for the promised land. The third is in form a supplication for Jerusalem, and it only 'qualifies' as a benediction by the closing *ḥatimah* ('Blessed are you . . .') which forms the end of each of the benedictions in the series. It is reasonable to suppose that such a tripartite form of benediction – thanksgiving – supplication was familiar in at least some Jewish circles at the beginning of the era, and that the primary contents of each benediction were already traditional.

In recent years a number of liturgical scholars have attempted to trace a linear development from this tripartite meal-blessing to the Christian Eucharistic Prayer. Finkelstein had already attempted to trace parallels between the *Birkath ha-mazon* and the prayers in *Didache* 10, and the Eucharistic Prayers of Hippolytus, *Apostolic Tradition*, and of Addai and Mari were now seen as further stages in this development.

Bouyer (1968, pp. 154–5) analyses his reconstruction of the Anaphora of Addai and Mari into three paragraphs, which he claims correspond to the three benedictions of the *Birkath ha-mazon*. Thus the first paragraph (Section B of our text) offers praise for creation, the second (Section D) gives thanks for redemption, and the third (a restored Institution Narrative followed by most of Sections G–I) contains the theme of memorial, and looks forward to the 'ultimate fulfilment in them of what is the object of the memorial'. A further detailed link between the second paragraph and the second benediction is found in the reference to 'knowledge' ('understanding' in l. 27 of our translation), which is held to correspond to the Jewish mention of the Torah. Even a cursory examination of the two texts reveals that these parallels are very widely drawn, and there is no specific correspondence of content.

Ligier (1973, pp. 176–85) further refines this approach by suggesting that the theme of glorification of the Creator who feeds all living creatures, which characterizes the first benediction of the *Birkath ha-mazon*, lost its importance in the Christian Eucharist after the separation of the latter from the Agape, and the theme of creation became absorbed into the second. This paves the way for retaining the theory of evolution from the *Birkath ha-mazon* while analysing the structure of the Anaphora of Addai and Mari into two rather than three parts. On pp. 174 f. Ligier adduces evidence from TB *Shabbath* 24a of discussions among rabbis of the second to fourth centuries about the insertion of festival commemorations (embolisms) into the *Birkath ha-mazon*. From these discussions it emerges that such embolisms might be made in either the second or the third benediction. This Ligier claims as a precedent for inserting an Institution Narrative into either the thanksgiving for redemption or the epicletic supplication. These are suggestive lines of thought, but as in the case of Bouyer's theory, are less than conclusive. Ligier's own comments on Bouyer's theory are worth noting: 'In short, theological or thematic similarities alone are not sufficient. In order to arrive at firm conclusions, it is necessary to pay attention to the form of the *berakoth* and to the total structures in which they are lodged' (p. 170).

Talley (1976, pp. 130–3) analyses the Anaphora of Addai and Mari, finding in it a tripartite pattern corresponding to the three benedictions of the *Birkath ha-mazon*. Three prayers of inclination (*gehanatha*) are each followed by a *qanona*, which functions as a doxology. Talley makes a distinction between praise for creation in the first *gehanta* (Section B and the beginning of Section C) and thanksgiving for redemption in the second (most of Section D), although he has to admit that this distinction is blurred by the mention of thanksgiving (l. 10) and redemption (l. 13) within the first *gehanta*. The third *gehanta* (Sections E–H and the beginning of I) with its memorial of the fathers recalls the Passover embolism in the third benediction of the *Birkath ha-mazon*. The anaphora as a whole thus reflects a tripartite structure praise – thanksgiving – supplication, where praise replaces blessing in the first element in the *Birkath ha-mazon*. The deceptive simplicity of this analysis, although based on a formal division as well as on a few select parallels of content, is belied by the inconsistency noted by Talley himself.

Other discussions may be mentioned more briefly. Sánchez Caro (1977) attempts to trace in the common core of the Anaphoras of Addai and Mari and *Sharar* three *gehanatha* modelled on the three benedictions of the *Birkath ha-mazon*, viz. Sections B, D, and E–F (largely following *Sharar* with an Institution Narrative) with I. He expresses some reservations about the correspondence of the third *gehanta* to the third benediction of the *Birkath ha-mazon*. Wegman (1979) offers a broadly similar reconstruction of the common core of the Anaphoras of Addai and Mari and *Sharar* (retaining Sections G and H, but incorporating an Institution Narrative in place of Section F). He differs from Ligier and Sánchez Caro in dividing the original core of this anaphora into four strophes, taking Section I as a separate concluding doxology corresponding to the *ḥatimah* at the end of the blessing of Jerusalem in the *Birkath ha-mazon*. Verheul (1980) too sees in the 'original' Anaphora of Addai and Mari four sections (B, D + G, H, and I) which he claims correspond to the three benedictions and final *ḥatimah* of the *Birkath ha-mazon*. He refers expressly to Wegman. These analyses are complicated by the positions adopted over the relationship between the Anaphora of Addai and Mari and *Sharar*, a question with which we shall be much concerned in the Commentary. No further details of correspondence with the content of the *Birkath ha-mazon* have been adduced.

The attempt to analyse the Anaphora of Addai and Mari into three sections (or four) corresponding to the benedictions of the *Birkath ha-mazon* must be adjudged a failure. In the first place some of the reconstructions of the 'original' anaphora to be analysed depend on the excisions of whole sections of the text, for which there is no evidence in the MS tradition and to which it is difficult to apply any external 'control'. In the second place division of the anaphora into sections by the *qanone* is misleading. In particular there is continuity between the *Sanctus* and its sequel, and it is difficult to claim any marked distinction of subject matter between Sections B and D. In the third place the parallels adduced with the contents of the *Birkath ha-mazon* are of the most general kind. Close verbal links are limited to the invitation 'Let us bless the Lord our God', which we argue in the Commentary underlies the present text of l. 7, and the formula 'And for all . . .' in ll. 31 and 60, which may represent genuine continuity with Jewish practice. Ironically the one part of the Anaphora of Addai and Mari that does have a close parallel in Jewish liturgical texts is the *Sanctus*, but this is not found at all in the *Birkath ha-mazon*. The suggestion that the anaphora is modelled expressly on the two benedictions preceding the recitation of the *Shemaʿ* in the morning service, where the *Sanctus* is found, is examined in the introduction to the Commentary and found to be no more convincing. In any case it has to be remembered that the *Sanctus* is biblical, and need not have been derived directly from Jewish liturgical forms at all.

In our present state of knowledge we can hardly go further than to say that there is evidence of the ultimate origin of Christian liturgical forms in Jewish forms, and some evidence of specific Jewish influence on Christian worship as late as the fourth century, but that the only specific common form that is not biblical in origin is the invitation 'Let us bless the Lord our God'. The paucity of specific evidence, together with the growing evidence both for pluriformity of practice and the absence of fixed forms in the first half of the first century, render the quest in Jewish liturgy for the content of the thanksgiving offered by Jesus at the Last Supper illusory. All we can say is that he was a Jew, and that there is some likelihood that his thanksgiving bore some resemblance to later Jewish forms of meal-blessing, while the latter may also have influenced some early Christians in the formation of their Eucharistic Prayers.

B. The Emergence of Fixed Forms in the Eucharistic Prayer

In a seminal article R. P. C. Hanson (1961) established that the freedom of the bishop to improvise the text of the Eucharistic Prayer persisted until at least the middle of the third century, and suggested that the absence of any extant complete liturgies dating from earlier than the middle of the fourth century probably indicates that there were few, if any, complete liturgies before the fourth century. Fenwick (1986) has drawn attention to the fascinating process by which anaphoras were constructed in the fourth century, while Bouley (1981) has attempted as complete an exploration as is possible on the basis of evidence currently available of the 'development of eucharistic prayer in the atmosphere of controlled freedom which marked the first three centuries' (p. xv). His conclusion is that 'Conventions governing the structure and content of improvised anaphoras are ascertainable in the second century and indicate that extempore prayer was not left merely to the whim of the minister. In the third century, and possibly even before, some anaphoral texts already existed in writing' (ibid).

While, as will be seen in the Commentary, it is not possible to prove that the earliest core of the Anaphora of Addai and Mari is as early as the beginning of the third century, there are certain indications that it may date from this period, and there is no conclusive evidence against such a dating. In this case this would be the earliest extant anaphora that enjoyed actual use in the early Church. There are substantial grounds for doubting whether the prayers in *Didache* 9–10 are eucharistic at all. The anaphora provided in Hippolytus, *Apostolic Tradition*, is clearly stated to be a model (and at at least one point reflects Hippolytus' own Logos doctrine). It is

clear that the bishop is free to compose his own anaphora, orthodoxy
of content being the only condition laid down, and the reproduction
of Hippolytus' text from memory is positively discouraged (ch. 9).
Hanson quotes Dix's translation of this passage (1968), including the
sentence: 'But if on the other hand he should pray and recite a prayer
according to a fixed form, no one should prevent him' (Dix's
translation actually reads 'shall' in place of 'should'). Cuming's
translation (1976), however, is preferable: 'But if anyone, when he
prays, utters a brief prayer, do not prevent him.' The meaning of 'in
mensura' is determined by the contrast with the preceding 'cum
sufficientia', and thus refers to the extent rather than to the freedom
of content of the prayer. The contrast is not between an extempore
and a fixed prayer, but between a long and a short one. The only
remaining complete anaphoral text before the second half of the
fourth century is that of Serapion's *Euchologion*. If this was the Bishop
of Thmuis's own composition for his own use, as seems most probable
(cf. Cuming, 1980), it will date at earliest from the beginning of his
episcopate *c.*339. The fact that the Anaphora of Addai and Mari
has affinities with those of both Hippolytus and Serapion and
probably dates from a period between them (see the Commentary)
suggests its importance as the earliest extant anaphora to have
attained a relatively fixed form for regular use in church.

In this section of the Introduction we are concerned with the
emergence of elements that were to become parts of the later fixed
anaphoral texts, but probably coexisted with a substantial amount of
improvisation in the late second and third centuries. It seems that too
definite a picture may have been drawn of the "conventions" the
bishop was expected to observe in composing his own anaphora. This
conception seems to derive from the conclusion of Hanson's discussion of an important, but obscure, statement of Origen in the *Dialogue
with Heracleides*, where he states (1961, p. 174): 'It is . . . clear that
there were "conventions" . . . which the bishop was expected, but
was not compelled, to use in composing his prayer.' Later in the
article he suggests that the traditional closing doxology was perhaps
one of the 'conventions', and that there was a conventional structure
for the Eucharistic Prayer as a whole. This term 'conventions' seems
to have caught the imagination of other scholars. Cuming (1975, p.
537), states (with explicit reference to Hanson): 'Origen refers to
certain conventions . . . within which the bishop was expected to
remain, even at that early date.' He goes on to enumerate ingredients

of the Eucharistic Prayer that were required by the 'conventions' at the time of Basil and Chrysostom. Fenwick (p. 8) follows in the same path, and seeks to interpret Basil's references to the unwritten tradition (on which see below) in this context. Bouley too (p. 141) speaks of 'liturgical conventions observed in praying the anaphora' and (p. 142) of 'Origen's explicit reference to credo-liturgical conventions'.

It is doubtful, however, whether the term συνθῆκαι can have the meaning of 'conventions', in the sense of 'accepted usages and customs' in which Hanson and his followers seem to use it. One is tempted to speculate whether Hanson may have been misled by Scherer's use of the French *conventions* to render the Greek word, though he clearly used the French word in the sense of 'agreement' or 'pact', which does correspond to one of the meanings of the Greek word. The question is of sufficient importance to make it necessary to examine the context of Origen's statement. Part of the relevant section of the text is corrupt beyond repair, but the most pertinent passages are:

Ἀεὶ προσφορὰ γίνεται θεῷ παντοκράτορι διὰ Ἰησοῦ Χριστοῦ, ὡς προσφόρου τῷ Πατρὶ τὴν θεότητα αὐτοῦ· μὴ δὶς ἀλλὰ Θεῷ διὰ Θεοῦ προσφορὰ γινέσθω. Τολμηρὸν δόξω λέγειν, εὐχόμενοι ἐμμένειν ταῖς συνθήκαις. . . . Εἰ δοκεῖ, αὗται αἱ συνθῆκαι γενέσθωσαν.
(Scherer, 1960, pp. 62, 64)

These may be translated:

The offering is always made to Almighty God through Jesus Christ, as related to the Father in respect of his divinity. Let the offering be made, not twice over, but to God through God. I shall seem to be speaking boldly: when praying we must abide by the agreements. . . . If it seems good to you, let these agreements be observed.

The context shows that Heracleides' Christology is under examination, and appeal is being made to the 'agreed usage' in the Eucharistic Prayer. The formula to which Origen appeals is essentially that of the preposition διά. It is 'through Christ' that the Eucharistic Prayer is addressed to the Father. Christ's role in the Eucharist is thus a mediatorial one, which he exercises in his divinity rather than in his humanity. Origen makes a play on προσφορά ('eucharistic offering') and προσφόρου in the description of Christ as 'related to' the Father in respect of his divinity. The Eucharist is offered not twice, to the Father and the Son separately, but once, to the Father through the Son, who is himself divine. The argument from liturgical usage thus reinforces the theological argument of the previous paragraph, that the Father and the Son are both divine and are one; that paragraph ended with a citation of John 10: 30.

The real importance of this passage for our purpose is the nature of the συνθῆκαι to which Origen appeals. In the primary edition of the text Scherer (1949) thought that this word referred to the agreements that were to be made as a practical conclusion to the Dialogue. Later, however, while still allowing this possibility, he expressed a preference for a more general reference to the agreed formulas of liturgical prayer (1960, p. 64, n. 1, accepting the arguments of Capelle, 1951, and Chadwick, 1954; Capelle suggests that the nature of the reference implies that it is to agreements already in force rather than to ones yet to be established, and Chadwick points out that Origen elsewhere uses this word of the promises and credal profession made in Baptism). Scherer indicates that the difficulty of determining the reference of the συνθῆκαι here is due to the lack of further specification, which is contrary to Origen's usage elsewhere; the reference must have been clear to the original audience, but it is no longer clear to us. The use of the word after the verb ἐμμένειν suggests a reference to some formal compact, treaty, or agreement (cf. Thucydides 5. 18. 9). One would almost be inclined to infer a reference to some earlier ruling like that of Canon 23 of the Council of Carthage (397), which required the Eucharistic Prayer to be addressed to the Father. The fact that such a canon was promulgated suggests that this was not universal practice at that time, but the force of Origen's argument here depends on his belief that this was the universal practice in his own time. There is no evidence of such an earlier ruling, although earlier evidence for the practice of offering the Eucharistic Prayer through Christ is to be found in Justin, 1 Apology 65. 3 and Dialogue with Trypho 117. 5, Hippolytus, Apostolic Tradition, Irenaeus, Adversus Haereses 4. 17. 6, and Tertullian, Adversus Marcionem 4. 9. 9. Capelle (1952, p. 168) argues that the appeal is in fact to the universal usage of the Church, which has the force of inviolable agreements, and Origen's language certainly suggests an acceptance of the obligation to use this particular formula. It may also be pertinent to recall Firmilian's reference to a female Montanist celebrant whose Eucharistic Prayer was 'non contemptibilis', yet was 'sine sacramento solitae praedicationis' (cit. Cyprian, *Epistle* 75. 10). Bouley's interpretation of 'solitae praedicationis' in this context as a Eucharistic Prayer formulated according to custom seems the most likely and, if so, this affords further evidence of 'binding traditions' in the composition of the Eucharistic Prayer.

The fact that Origen uses the plural συνθῆκαι suggests that he is appealing to an obligation to more than a single observance. Yet his specific appeal is to the address of the Eucharistic Prayer to the Father through (διά) the Son, and it is doubtful whether this passage can be regarded as evidence for any other specific usage. This after all is the one point emphasized twice in the context, and the one directly relevant to Origen's argument at this point. Is it possible to infer from his other writings any further specific usages that form part of these inviolable traditions? It is sometimes suggested that Origen refers to the *epiklēsis*. Yet it is doubtful whether any of the passages adduced attest anything more specific than the concept of consecration by the Eucharistic Prayer as a whole, which is found already in Justin (Gelston, 1982, pp. 174 f.). In his *Commentary on Matt.* 11. 14 Origen refers to the 'bread sanctified by the word of God and prayer', which seems to be a direct allusion to 1 Tim. 4: 5, and later in the same passage he states: 'What is of benefit is the word uttered over it [sc. the bread].' Similarly in *Contra Celsum* 8. 33 he says that the bread 'has become a body consecrated by the prayer'. In his *Commentary on 1 Cor.* 7. 5 he refers to bread 'over which the name of God and of Christ and of the Holy Spirit has been invoked'. Bouley's suggestion (p. 139) that the reference is to a Eucharistic Prayer in which all three Persons are named, 'perhaps an allusion to some form of primitive trinitarian structure of the prayer and to its final doxology' seems the most likely. It is precarious then to infer from these passages any evidence of a traditional formula for the *epiklēsis*, or indeed anything more specific than the general conception of consecration by the use of the Eucharistic Prayer. We conclude then that, while Origen shows awareness of a number of binding traditions of liturgical usage, the only specific information we can derive from his writings about the Eucharistic Prayer is that it is addressed to the Father through (διά) the Son.

If we can derive little concrete information from Origen's reference to the συνθῆκαι, can we glean more from a passage not directly discussed in Hanson's review of the evidence? This occurs in Basil of Caesarea's *De Spiritu Sancto* 27. 66, dating from AD 375. Basil is dealing here with two kinds of apostolic tradition, one of which is recorded in the New Testament, while the other is non-scriptural. Amand de Mendieta (1965, pp. 21–39) has demonstrated that this, rather than the distinction between written and oral tradition, is the key to the interpretation of the terms ἐγγράφως and ἀγράφου. Among examples of non-scriptural tradition are parts of the Eucharistic Prayer. Basil's argument is that forms of the Trinitarian doxology in which the Holy Spirit is introduced by the preposition σύν are well attested, and that the doctrine of the divine equality of the Holy Spirit with the Father and the Son is thus rooted in tradition. We are concerned here not with the wider aspects of this question or with the use Basil makes of this argument in affirming the divinity of the Holy Spirit, but simply with the historical evidence for the content of the Eucharistic Prayer to be derived from this passage. The relevant section reads:

Τὰ τῆς ἐπικλήσεως ῥήματα ἐπὶ τῇ ἀναδείξει τοῦ ἄρτου τῆς Εὐχαριστίας καὶ τοῦ ποτηρίου τῆς εὐλογίας, τίς τῶν ἁγίων ἐγγράφως ἡμῖν καταλέλοιπεν; Οὐ γὰρ δὴ τούτοις ἀρκούμεθα, ὧν ὁ ἀπόστολος ἢ τὸ εὐαγγέλιον ἐπεμνήσθη, ἀλλὰ καὶ προλέγομεν καὶ ἐπιλέγομεν ἕτερα, ὡς μεγάλην ἔχοντα πρὸς τὸ μυστήριον τὴν ἰσχὺν, ἐκ τῆς ἀγράφου διδασκαλίας παραλαβόντες.

Some comments are required before we can offer a translation. In particular it is necessary to attempt to determine the sense of ἐπίκλησις in this passage. Amand de Mendieta (p. 2, n. 3) argues that the word is used here not in the technical sense of an invocation of the Holy Spirit on the worshippers and the eucharistic elements, but in the more general sense of 'invocation' with reference to the Eucharistic Prayer as a whole. In particular he points to the γάρ at the beginning of the second sentence. Bouley (pp. 237 f., n. 100) tends independently to the same conclusion. While it is clear that the word ἐπίκλησις can be used of the Eucharistic Prayer as a whole (Lampe, 1961, s.v., 4), the present context suggests that this is unlikely to be its meaning here. Basil refers specifically to τὰ τῆς ἐπικλήσεως ῥήματα ἐπὶ τῇ ἀναδείξει τοῦ ἄρτου τῆς Εὐχαριστίας καὶ τοῦ ποτηρίου τῆς εὐλογίας. The use of the cognate verb ἀναδεῖξαι in the Liturgy of Basil (*LEW*, 1965, p. 327, l. 29, and p. 329, l. 32; cf. Lampe, s.v., for references in other liturgies) points rather in the direction of the specific invocation of the Holy Spirit on the elements for the purpose of consecration (so already Fortescue,

1912, p. 114). This more specific sense of ἐπίκλησις finds support in the analogy drawn between the invocation of the Holy Spirit on the eucharistic elements and on the anointing oil used in chrismation by Cyril of Jerusalem (*Cat. Myst.* 3. 3, cf. *Cat.* 3. 3 for a similar reference to the consecration of the baptismal water).

In the following sentence Basil refers to the fact that the content of the Eucharistic Prayer is not restricted to what is recorded by the Apostle or the Gospel, i.e. the Institution Narrative, but that this is both preceded and followed by other material derived from the non-scriptural tradition. It is of course possible that Basil refers here to the whole of the Eucharistic Prayer. In view, however, of his awareness of different forms of doxology, and of his evident readiness to revise earlier forms of the anaphora, he can hardly be claiming that the whole of the anaphora derives from apostolic, but non-scriptural, tradition. It seems more likely that he is referring simply to certain components of the Eucharistic Prayer that were by his time traditional. In this case the second sentence amplifies the argument of the preceding question to include other traditional elements in the Eucharistic Prayer besides the ἐπίκλησις in the technical sense.

We may now offer a translation:

Which of the saints has left us in Scripture the words of the Invocation at the consecration of the bread of the Eucharist and of the cup of blessing? For we are not content with these things that the Apostle or the Gospel mention, but we say other things before and after, as having great importance for the sacrament, having received them from the non-scriptural teaching.

If this interpretation is right, it is pertinent to speculate which particular traditional elements of the Eucharistic Prayer Basil may have had in mind. Amand de Mendieta (p. 3, n. 1) suggests the following elements before the Institution Narrative: the opening dialogue, the Preface, the *Sanctus*, and the extensive thanksgiving. After the Institution Narrative he suggests the *anamnēsis*, the *epiklēsis*, perhaps the Great Intercession, and the final doxology. This estimate is probably too high. We may be reasonably confident that the opening dialogue and the *Sanctus* (attested already respectively in Hippolytus and Serapion) were traditional by this time. If our interpretation of the passage quoted above is correct, we have Basil's own testimony that the *epiklēsis* was traditional, and this is supported by the presence of some form of *epiklēsis* in both Hippolytus and Serapion. As for the doxology, it must be noted that Basil himself attests the use of different formulae of doxology (*De Spiritu Sancto* 1. 3):

Προσευχομένῳ μοί πρῴην μετὰ τοῦ λαοῦ, καὶ ἀμφοτέρως τὴν δοξολογίαν ἀποπληροῦντι τῷ θεῷ καὶ Πατρί, νῦν μὲν μετὰ τοῦ Υἱοῦ σὺν τῷ Πνεύματι τῷ ἁγίῳ, νῦν δὲ διὰ τοῦ Υἱοῦ ἐν τῷ ἁγίῳ Πνεύματι, ἐπέσκηψάν τινες τῶν παρόντων, ξενιζούσαις ἡμᾶς φωναῖς κεχρῆσθαι λέγοντες, καὶ ἅμα πρὸς ἀλλήλας ὑπεναντίως ἐχούσαις.

To this text may be added the citation of the doxology used by Dionysius of Alexandria given by Basil later in the same work (*De Spiritu Sancto* 29. 72):

Τῷ δὲ Θεῷ Πατρὶ καὶ Υἱῷ τῷ Κυρίῳ ἡμῶν Ἰησοῦ Χριστῷ σὺν τῷ ἁγίῳ Πνεύματι δόξα καὶ κράτος εἰς τοὺς αἰῶνας τῶν αἰώνων, ἀμήν.

This doxology Dionysius introduces as a 'model' (τύπον) and 'rule' (κανόνα) received from earlier presbyters, which he himself uses in concluding his own Eucharistic Prayer. These terms suggest that he regarded it as a sacrosanct tradition, at least in Alexandria. Hanson (p. 175) reasonably infers: 'The fact that Dionysius emphasizes that he ends his prayer with a fixed formula may perhaps imply that the rest of the prayer is not fixed.' On the other hand Basil himself, on his own admission, varied the precise wording of his own doxology, and neither of his own formulas agrees with that of Dionysius. This degree of variation suggests that any specific doxological formula was regarded as fixed and binding at most in a given locality, and perhaps that what was regarded as a generally binding tradition was no more than that the closing doxology of the Eucharistic Prayer should be Trinitarian in its formulation.

As for the other elements in the Eucharistic Prayer suggested by Amand de Mendieta, it is unlikely that by this time tradition required anything like a fixed form, although the presence of elements of this nature was probably by now required, except perhaps for the intercessions which seem from Cyril of Jerusalem's self-conscious exposition (*Cat. Myst.* 5. 8–10) to be a fairly recent introduction in the anaphora itself. Fenwick has drawn attention to the probable extent of Basil's own creative contributions to the development of the anaphora, and these would only be possible at a period when even written texts were not regarded as final and inalterable. It is likely that certain expressions were becoming customary, perhaps particularly in the immediate introduction to the

Sanctus and in the *anamnēsis* (for which again cf. Hippolytus), but we
can hardly hope to determine precisely which elements in his
Eucharistic Prayer Basil himself regarded as deriving from non-
scriptural, but apostolic, tradition. That there was still in Basil's time
considerable scope for freedom in formulating the content of the
Eucharistic prayer is clear not only from the indirect evidence of his
own liturgical creativity, but also from the criticisms and advice he
offers. For instance, in his *Constitutiones Monasticae* 1. 2 (*PG* 31.
1329A) he writes:

ὅταν δοξολογήσῃς αὐτόν, μὴ πλανώμενος τὸν νοῦν ὧδε καὶ ἐκεῖσε, μηδὲ
Ἑλληνικῶς μυθολογῶν, ἀλλ᾽ ἀπὸ τῶν ἁγίων Γραφῶν ἐκλεγόμενος.

When you praise him, not wandering in mind hither and thither, or telling
mythical tales in a Greek manner, but selecting [sc. material] from the Holy
Scriptures.

This implies that many Eucharistic Prayers were diffuse and dis-
orderly, and that their subject matter was too little derived from
Scripture. The contrast with Greek mythology is probably to be
explained in the light of other passages (*PG* 31. 253C and 913A, cf.
also *De Spiritu Sancto* 8. 18). Here Basil deplores excessive concentration on the lesser benefits of creation when the saving acts of God
ought primarily to engage our thanksgiving (See Cuming, 1981,
p.11). If Basil can thus try to influence the proportions of the
thanksgiving and the source from which its contents are drawn, it is
clear that there is still very considerable scope for creativity. The
general picture then that emerges from Basil's testimony is that of a
still fluid form of Eucharistic Prayer in which nevertheless some
elements have become traditional (although not always in an
identical or fixed form).

  It is useful to compare what Bouley (p. 232) writes about the
anaphora of *Apostolic Constitutions* 8:

The text indicates that at the end of the fourth century core sections of
the anaphora, like the institution account, anamnesis and epiclesis, were
quite stereotyped. The *oratio theologia*, however, might vary greatly
through freer improvisation, while the intercessions were still in the process of development. It indicates too, that a written model might be
produced which would influence extempore prayer if such still existed and
serve also as a source for the composition or amplification of other written
anaphoras.

The term *oratio theologia* is explained earlier (p. 221, n. 16) as 'a convenient way of referring to the first part of eastern anaphoras prior to the *sanctus* (or the intercessions in the Alexandrian type) in the fully developed prayers or to the opening sections of praise and thanksgiving in earlier exemplars'. With this may be compared his discussion (pp. 166 f.) of Augustine's response to Petilianus, in which he concludes, with Frere, that the prayer of the priest ('precem sacerdotis verbis et mysteriis evangelicis conformatam') refers to the Institution Narrative and constitutes no evidence that the entire Eucharistic Prayer was a fixed formula in Africa at the beginning of the fifth century. He goes on to point out that the opening dialogue and the Institution Narrative were also the only invariable parts of the Eucharistic Prayer in the Spanish and Gallican rites.

We also need to bear in mind some recent warnings about the extent to which it is possible to reconstruct a primitive, and supposedly normative, form of the Eucharistic Prayer, or realistic to suppose that such a form ever existed. Spinks (1985, pp. 217–19), draws attention to the paucity of the evidence available for the earliest period, and the need for caution in its evaluation:

the evidence upon which to construct an hypothesis of anaphoral development is extremely limited. . . . the result is but a few pieces of a vast jigsaw. Apart from these few pieces, the rest is lost. To guess what the full picture might have been on the basis of these few pieces is indeed hazardous. (pp. 217 f.)

In the light of a consideration of recent developments in Jewish liturgical scholarship, Bradshaw (1987) writes (p. 31):

In spite of the transformation which has taken place in New Testament studies in recent years in recognizing the fundamental pluriformity of early Christianity, there has still been a residual tendency in liturgical scholarship to look for the most ancient stratum in those elements which are common to all, or nearly all, later texts, rather than in those which are distinctive of individual traditions, and in particular to seek to trace the evolution of all eucharistic prayers from a single root.

Can we then hope realistically to determine at all which elements of the Eucharistic Prayer were beginning to become even relatively fixed at about the beginning of the third century? We may perhaps suggest tentatively that there were three kinds of element that showed an early tendency towards fixity. The first kind is the one that consists essentially of scriptural material, and comprises the

Sanctus, the Institution Narrative, and the closing congregationa[l] *Amen* (cf. 1 Cor. 14: 16). Even though differing forms of the first two are found over a long period, it is reasonable to suppose that local usage would tend towards fixity at an earlier, rather than a later, date. The first and last of these elements overlap with the second kind, that involving congregational participation. For this to be practicable at all, the congregational response needs to be fixed and the cue introducing it to be at least recognizably familiar. Here we think of the opening dialogue, the immediate prelude to the *Sanctus*, and the concluding doxology. Again there is ample evidence of differences in detail, but we are also aware of the emergence of stereotyped phrases, and practical exigency must have conduced to at least a degree of local consistency. The third kind of element is more difficult to define and shows less evidence of attaining an early fixed form. This consists of what at least came to be thought of as emanating from very early tradition. One thinks of such evidence as the allusions of Justin to the themes of the eucharistic thanksgiving, the 'binding tradition' alluded to by Origen that the Eucharistic Prayer be addressed to the Father through the Son, and the *epiklēsis* attested by Basil. When we compare this list of elements, which may reasonably be supposed to have been moving towards fixity at the beginning of the third century, with the material in the Appendix in which we attempt to determine the oldest strata in the Anaphora of Addai and Mari we find that the only elements missing in the latter are the Institution Narrative and the explicit offering of the anaphora to the Father *through* Christ. Even these elements, however, though not verbally present, may be held to be implicit in the oldest strata of this ancient anaphora. Despite all the obscurities in detail, the Anaphora of Addai and Mari emerges as a text of prime importance for the history of the evolution of the Eucharistic Prayer.

C. The Eucharistic Prayer in the East Syrian tradition

The origins of East Syrian Christianity are lost in obscurity. The division of East Syrians from West Syrians was the result of the Christological controversies of the fifth century, and was precipitated in particular by the Council of Ephesus in AD 431. In the second half of the century the Monophysites came to prevail in Edessa, and the

East Syrians who followed the teachings of Theodore of Mopsuestia withdrew into Persia. Nisibis became the main East Syrian theological centre. Political factors contributed largely to the subsequent isolation of the East Syrian Church from the rest of Christendom for a long period.

Antioch has the distinction of being the place where followers of Christ were first called 'Christians' (Acts 11: 26), and its evangelization is recorded in the Acts of the Apostles. It is, however, unlikely that the origins of East Syrian Christianity are to be traced directly to Antioch. The sixth-century *Doctrine of Addai* (Phillips–Howard 1876, 1981) records the charming legend of King Abgar's letter to Jesus asking him to come and heal him, and Jesus' reply that his work here was now finished, but that after his Ascension he would send one of his disciples. After the Ascension Judas Thomas sent Addai, one of the seventy-two (Luke 10: 1), who evangelized Edessa. Lane (1981) points out the inconsistencies and anachronisms in this legend, including the confusion of two kings of the name Abgar, one of the first century and the other of the late second century. His judgement is worth quoting:

On the face of it, there is a late second-century Christianity trying to justify itself to others with traditions linking it with the churches of Antioch and of Rome, and to justify itself to itself with traditions taking it back not only to the first years of Christianity but also to the time of our Lord himself, even before the crucifixion. (p. 109)

Lane goes on to offer reasons for suspecting that elements of other stories have been incorporated into the Addai narrative, one of which concerned the adoption of Judaism by the kingdom of Adiabene. A further detail is that on the death of Addai's successor Aggai, Paluṭ went to Antioch to be ordained priest by Bishop Serapion of Antioch. This suggests a genuine reminiscence of at least an early connection of East Syrian Christianity with Antioch.

The complexities of the early history of East Syrian Christianity cannot be explored further here (see Lane, 1981; Murray, 1975, pp. 4–24, for brief treatments; and Segal, 1970, Ch. 3, for a fuller account of the Church at Edessa). Only three further points need to be made for our purposes. One is that the Anaphora of Addai and Mari is named after Addai, the traditional apostle of Edessa, and Mari his disciple. In fact the earliest texts of the anaphora are entitled simply ܩܘܕܫܐ ܕܫܠܝܚܐ ('The Sanctification of the

Apostles'), and it is sometimes suggested that the original reference was to the twelve apostles, the identification with Addai and Mari being secondary. The real import of the title is to claim apostolic origin for the anaphora. The second point is that the demonstration of the existence of a common core to this anaphora and the Maronite anaphora *Sharar* (see the Commentary, introduction and *passim*) proves that such a core must antedate the divisions of the fifth century and thus belong to the earlier unified tradition of Syrian eucharistic liturgy.

The third point that needs to be made here is a reminder of the close contact of the early Syrian Church with Judaism. 'Scholars are recognizing more and more the Jewish character of Syrian Christianity and the intimate contacts between church and synagogue in Syria (Fiensy, p. 217). Fiensy documents this for Antioch in the second, third, and fourth centuries. The Semitic flavour of the Anaphora of Addai and Mari is a further indication of this. So are such other liturgical features as the reading on many occasions of two Old Testament lections in the synaxis (Jammo, 1979, p. 108; cf. the readings from the Law and Prophets in *Apostolic Constitutions* 8. 5. 11, and synagogue practice as recorded in Acts 13: 15), and the reading of these lections from a raised platform in the centre of the church called the *bēma*, which is analogous to that of the synagogue.

Macomber (1977a) records some interesting historical data, some of which present problems of interpretation. On p. 109 he quotes Canon 13 from the first general synod of the Church of Persia in AD 410: 'Now and henceforward we will all with one accord celebrate the liturgy according to the western rite, which the Bishops Isaac and Marutha have taught us, and which we have seen them celebrate here in the church of Seleucia' (pp. 27 and 266 in Chabot's 1902 edition). Unfortunately it is not possible to identify the rite in question. On p. 111 Macomber discusses the tradition that Mar Aba I, before he became patriarch in 540, secured Greek texts of the anaphoras attributed to Theodore of Mopsuestia and Nestorius, which were subsequently translated into Syriac and came into use in the East Syrian Church alongside the anaphora of Addai and Mari. Spinks (1984b, p. 355) quotes late MS headings for this tradition. In the case of Nestorius we may add the evidence of Ebedjesu (Assemani, 3. 1. 20), who notes that this is a lengthy anaphora. For Theodore Ebedjesu (ibid. 19) mentions no anaphora, but only a book on the sacraments, which, along with the book on the faith mentioned immediately afterwards, is probably to be identified with Theodore's catechetical and mystagogical lectures. On pp. 112 f. Macomber discusses the reforms of the patriarch Isho'yabh III (650–9), including the assignment of the three anaphoras to specific liturgical days. This seems to preclude the further use of a fourth anaphora, of Chrysostom, mentioned by Ibn aṭ-Ṭayib as authorized by 'the fathers' (CSCO 167–8, pp. 90 and 93), or indeed that of Ephrem mentioned in the *Chronicle of Seert* (PO 4. 295) or those of Narsai and Barsauma mentioned by Ebedjesu (Assemani 3. 1, chs. 53–4), if these traditions are well founded. It seems that the East Syrian anaphoral tradition was richer and more varied in the period before Isho'yabh's reforms. The tradition that Isho'yabh abbreviated the Anaphora of Addai and Mari is discussed in the introduction to the Commentary, where the difficulties of reconciling it with the existence of the common core of the Anaphoras of Addai and Mari and *Sharar* before AD 431 are noted.

Critical editions of the Anaphoras of Nestorius and Theodore are not yet available, and it is not necessary for our purposes to examine them in detail. It is in any case unwise to attempt any detailed study of these anaphoras before critical texts become available. It is interesting, for instance, that the text of the opening dialogue in the Anaphora of Theodore (though not in that of Nestorius) is identical with that in the Anaphora of Addai and Mari in the Mar Esh'aya text, and does not contain the festal additions in Kelaita's text (1928) which are printed as part of the normative text in the Anglican edition of Urmia. The origins of these two anaphoras are still beset by uncertainties. Spinks (1984*b*, pp. 353–7) gives a summary of what is known, indicating a possible date in the second or third decade of the sixth century, and noting the improbability of either anaphora having been actually composed by the father after whom it is named.

Spinks refers to studies of Bayard Jones, Botte, and Wagner, which indicate that the Anaphora of Nestorius is a skilful conflation of material from those of Basil and Chrysostom (or the Twelve Apostles) and that of Addai and Mari. The question of a possible link between l. 51 of the Anaphora of Addai and Mari and the introduction to the *epiklēsis* in that of Nestorius is discussed in the Commentary on Section G.

Brightman (1930) quotes parallels in Theodore's writings in an attempt to substantiate his authorship of the anaphora named after him. The tradition that Theodore composed an anaphora is as old as

Leontius of Byzantium (*PG* 86. 1368c), but the anaphora on which Theodore comments in his *Mystagogical Lecture* 16 can hardly be identified with the East Syrian anaphora attributed to him. Spinks (1984*a*, p. 66) refers to a paper of the late Douglas Webb (1990) in which it is argued that some of the material in the Anaphora of Theodore is derived from that of Nestorius. The parallels between ll. 41, 43–6 of the Anaphora of Addai and Mari and the corresponding passage in that of Theodore are discussed in the Commentary on Sections E–F, where the conclusion is reached that the prior form is probably that of Addai and Mari. The parallel between ll. 51 and 54 of the Anaphora of Addai and Mari and the *anamnēsis* in that of Theodore is discussed in the Commentary on Section G, where it is argued that this does not constitute a basis for a theory of an original Institution Narrative in the Anaphora of Addai and Mari.

The posthumous studies of Bayard H. Jones (1964–6) sought to establish that the Anaphora of Addai and Mari was a later abridgement of that of Nestorius. This theory is belied by the demonstration of the existence of a common core of the Anaphoras of Addai and Mari and *Sharar* at a period before the Council of Ephesus in AD 431. For more detailed discussion of this theory see Galvin (1973, pp. 401–5) and Mannooramparampil (1984, pp. 10–15).

The bearing of the sixth-century fragment of an anaphora edited by Connolly (1925) on the text of that of Addai and Mari is discussed fully in the Commentary. It is not possible at present to relate it directly to the extant historical traditions, but in the nature of its allusion to the Institution it more closely resembles the Anaphora of Addai and Mari than those of Nestorius and Theodore, which both have a full Institution Narrative in the normal sense of the term.

It is reasonable to attempt to supplement the information to be derived from the historical notices and the anaphoral texts themselves with what may be inferred from the early commentaries. We shall confine our attention to the three oldest (see Macomber, 1977*b*, pp. 525–8, with a brief account of later ones on pp. 528–30).

Theodore of Mopsuestia's *Mystagogical Lecture* 16 includes an account of the anaphora (pp. 96–123 and 234–65 in Mingana's 1933 edition). Macomber (1977*b*, pp. 525 f.) classifies this as an Antiochene anaphora, but considers that it may have influenced the

Chaldaean liturgy. Bouley (p. 235) draws attention to the evident West Syrian form of this anaphora, and to the fact that it has little in common with the Anaphora of Theodore used in the East Syrian Church. He cites further studies which cannot be discussed here. A convenient summary of the information about the content of the anaphora to be gleaned from Theodore's lecture may be found in *PEER* (pp. 135–7). See further Lietzmann (1933) for an analysis and critique of these data. Unfortunately the verbatim quotations are few, and it is possible to reconstruct only the general outline and content of the anaphora. The direct quotations include the opening dialogue, the *Sanctus*, and the beginning of the post-*Sanctus*: 'Holy is the Father, holy also is the Son, and holy also the Holy Spirit' (Mingana, pp. 102 and 242), but it is clear that the anaphora contains an Institution Narrative and an *epiklēsis* and concludes with intercessions for the living and the departed. Because of the importance of the quotations of the opening dialogue and the *Sanctus* in Theodore's lecture (which survives only in a Syriac translation) for the Syriac text of these passages at an early date, they are taken into consideration in the Commentary on Sections A and C of the Anaphora of Addai and Mari. For our purposes the most interesting material is the opening dialogue, especially the remarkable agreement with the Anaphora of Addai and Mari in the response to the *Sursum corda*.

An account of the anaphora is also given in Narsai's *Homily* 17. Ratcliff (1963) in an imaginative and stimulating study suggested that while the anaphora presupposed in *Homily* 17 'represents the historic East Syrian anaphoral tradition revised in such a way as to bring it into closer accord with Greek models', two earlier anaphoras can be detected in *Homilies* 21 and 32. Spinks (1980b), however, has shown good reasons for believing that Narsai makes only selective reference to the anaphora in *Homilies* 21 and 32, and that the anaphoral text presupposed in all three homilies is the same. The exposition of the anaphora in *Homily* 17 (pp. 11–23 in Connolly's 1909 edition) again yields very little by way of direct quotation from the text. Only the opening dialogue and the *Sanctus* with its immediate prelude are explicitly quoted, probably because these would have been the only parts of the anaphora audible to the initiates. Even the quotations of the opening dialogue do not correspond exactly to the text of any of the three extant anaphoras, and one is inclined to think that the mystagogue is freely mingling text and interpretation. Spinks (1984*b*, p. 356) makes the reasonable point that 'if Narsai was commenting upon the anaphora *in general*, when his Church used at least three, then it is understandable that his comments do not correspond exactly to the contents of one particular anaphora.' He goes on to trace specific parallels with the anaphoras of both Theodore and Nestorius. On the essential authenticity of this homily see Macomber (1977*b*, pp. 526 f.) and Jammo (1979, pp. 13–25). Two further details may be noted, although they cannot be explored further here. The Institution Narrative (Connolly, 1909, pp. 16 f.) contains what purports to be the content of Jesus' own thanksgiving at the Last Supper, and this prayer has been claimed (Macomber, 1975–6) as an anaphora composed by Theodore; Narsai attributes it directly to Theodore. The summary of the intercessions is explicitly said to be in imitation of Mar Nestorius (Connolly, 1909, p. 20). It is interesting that the intercessions precede the *epiklēsis*, as in the three extant East Syrian anaphoras, and in contrast to the anaphora expounded in Theodore's *Mystagogical Lecture* 16, where as we have seen the *epiklēsis* precedes the intercessions.

The commentary of Gabriel Qatraya on the East Syrian liturgical rites was dated by Jammo (1966) in the early seventh century, before the reforms of the patriarch Isho'yabh III. In a penetrating study Spinks (1984*a*) has drawn attention to the impossibility of determining which anaphoral text forms the basis of this commentary. A passing reference to the mysteries being performed in memory 'of the passion, and death and resurrection of our Lord' may be an allusion to l. 55 of the Anaphora of Addai and Mari, which has no parallel in the *anamnēsis* of Theodore or Nestorius, but, as Spinks points out, the phrase could equally well have been derived from a pre-anaphoral prayer in Theodore and Nestorius. He points out further that Qatraya's Institution Narrative could be dependent on that in the Anaphora of Theodore, while the verb that Qatraya uses for the descent of the Holy Spirit at the *epiklēsis* (the Aph'el of ܐ, 'overshadow') is used only in the Anaphora of Theodore. While Spinks is certainly correct in saying that it is impossible to determine the anaphoral text that forms the basis of Qatraya's commentary, the most positive indications suggest that it is that of Theodore rather than those of Addai and Mari or Nestorius.

The modifications of the Anaphora of Addai and Mari in the Chaldaean and Malabar liturgies, while significant in their own right, belong properly to the period later than that of the medieval text of the anaphora that we have sought to establish. Some details are noted in the material on the text and MSS, but they are unlikely to be relevant to the quest for the earlier form of the anaphora, which is the main purpose of the Commentary.

It remains only to indicate the relation of the Anaphora of Addai and Mari to the Syrian anaphoral tradition as a whole. The West Syrian anaphoral tradition has probably been influenced by practices derived from Egypt and Jerusalem. While there is some evidence of the influence of Greek anaphoras in those of Nestorius and Theodore, possibly mediated at least in part through the *Mystagogical Lecture* 16 of Theodore himself, the Semitic character of the Anaphora of Addai and Mari has often been remarked. The few parallels with the Anaphora of Chrysostom are noted in the introduction to the Commentary, where it is suggested that they reflect a distant relationship between the two anaphoras within the wider Syrian 'family'. The existence of a common core of the Anaphoras of Addai and Mari and *Sharar* proves that the former is not an exclusive product of the separate East Syrian tradition, but is older than the divisions arising from the christological controversies of the fifth century. Several factors are suggestive of a date around the beginning of the third century (see the introduction to the Commentary). If this is correct, the Anaphora of Addai and Mari is almost certainly the oldest extant anaphora within the Syrian tradition, and very probably the traditional Anaphora of Edessa (cf. Macomber, 1973). Its importance for the history of the development of the Christian Eucharistic Prayer can hardly be exaggerated.

THE TEXT

The Manuscripts

THE list of extant MSS given here and known to contain the text of Addai and Mari makes no claim to be complete. It is, with a few additions, a conflation of the lists compiled by Macomber (1966) and Webb (1967–8), rearranged in as consistent a chronological order as seems possible, MSS assigned merely to a century being listed before those of the same century to which a more specific date can be given. Of the fifty-three MSS listed by Macomber and the fifty-seven listed by Webb thirty-five are common to their two lists, so that seventy-five of the eighty-six MSS listed below derive from either or both of these lists.

The eleven MSS in the list that figure in neither of the previous lists fall into two categories:

(a) five MSS newly collated in the preparation of this edition:
  11, 41: mentioned by Macomber (1966, pp. 343, 355, n. 1).
  28: collated by Webb in his contribution to Spinks's 1980 edition.
  78: mentioned in a note in the Webb Archive.
  85: another text in the McHardy Codex in addition to the one collated by Macomber.

(b) six MSS to which reference is made in published works:
  26, 76, 80: see J. Vosté: *Catalogue de la Bibliothèque Syro-Chaldéenne du couvent de Notre-Dame des Semences près d'Alqoš (Iraq)*, (Rome–Paris, 1929). MSS in this catalogue later than 1850 have not been included in the list below.
  29: described by E. R. Hambye in *Mémorial Mgr. Gabriel Khouri-Sarkis* (Louvain, 1969, pp. 221–31), but not yet published to the knowledge of the present editor.
  52: mentioned by Webb in Spinks's 1980 edition (p. 31), and verified in Zotenberg's catalogue.
  53: mentioned by Macomber (1966, pp. 343–4). According

to a note in the Webb Archive this MS does contain the text
of Addai and Mari.

The list contains:

(a) a new serial number;

(b) the place where each MS is held, together with its catalogue
number if available, and a note of the folio or page references
to the text of the Eucharistic Prayer of Addai and Mari;

(c) the date of the MS or an approximation to it;

(d) a classification where possible into one of five categories (on
which see below): Ḥudra (see p. 35 below), Alqosh (Webb's
Group A), Webb B (Webb's Group B), Chaldaean, and
Malabar;

(e) the siglum assigned in Macomber (1966, pp. 354–6);

(f) the serial number assigned in Webb (1967–8, pp. 522–3);

(g) the siglum assigned to twelve MSS not included in
Macomber's apparatus from which readings were added by
Webb to the apparatus in Spinks's 1980 edition; the list of sigla
is on p. 15.

MANUSCRIPTS OF ADDAI AND MARI

				Macomber	Webb	Spinks
1	Mar Esh'aya, Mosul, fos. 4^r–5^r	10th c.	Ḥudra	Basic Text	1	
2	Diarbekir (Mardin-Diarbekir 31.47), fos. 208^v–211^r	12th c.	Ḥudra	A	2	
3	Mardin 22, fos. 327^v–329r	1287	Hudra	B	3	
4	Cambridge Add. 2046B, fos. 106^v–108^r, 136^v, 133	15th c.	Webb-B	C	8	
5	Diarbekir 48, fos. 5^v–9^v	15th c.		D	7	
6	Mardin 19, fos. 36^v–41^v	15th c.		E	5	

				Macomber	Webb	Spinks
7	Baghdad, CP 333, fos. 12ʳ–13ᵛ	15th c.	Ḥudra	F	9	
8	London, BL Or. 5750, fos. 7ᵛ–8ʳ	15th c.	Ḥudra	G	10	
9	Berlin 38 (Sachau 167), fos. 87ᵛ–91ᵛ	1496	Webb-B	H	11	
10	Baghdad CP 36, fos. 4ᵛ–8ʳ	15/16th c.	Webb-B	I	17	
11	Berlin 47 (Sachau 354), fos. 98ᵛ–100ᵛ	15/16th c.	Ḥudra			
12	Rouen Or. 21, fos. 32ᵛ–36ᵛ	16th c.	Webb-B	K	12	
13	Saigh Ḥudra (fragment)	16th c.	Ḥudra	L		
14	London BL Or. 4060, fo. 1 (fragment)	16th c.		M		
15	Rome, Vat. Borg. Syr. 150, pp. 521–2	16th c.	Ḥudra	N	13	
16	Rome, Vat. Syr. 66, fos. 104ᵛ–107ᵛ	c.1558	Webb-B	O	14	
17	Alqosh 70, pp. 3–6	1564	Webb-B	P	15	
18	Mardin 20 (fragment)	1566		Q	6	
19	London, BL Add. 7181, fos. 34ᵛ–37ᵛ (incomplete)	1570	Alqosh	R	16	
20	N.–D. des Semences 92	1578	Alqosh	S		
21	Mardin Ritual (Mardin-Diarbekir 33.23)	1584/5		T		
22	Baghdad, CP 40, pp. 47–57	1600	Alqosh	U	20	
23	Baghdad, CP 209, pp. 5–11	16/17th c.	Alqosh	V	18	
24	Berlin 39 (Or. Quart. 804), fos. 20ʳ–24ʳ	17th c.	Webb-B	J	19	

				Macomber	Webb	Spinks
25	Woodbrooke, Ming. Syr. 611, fos. 68^v–72^r	17th c.	Malabar	Z		
26	N.–D. des Semences 94	17th c.				
27	Rome, Vat. Syr. 42, fos. 33^v–37^r	1603	Alqosh	W	21	
28	Manchester, Rylands Syr. 19, fos. 13^r–18^r	1604				a
29	Lisbon, Ajuda 52-VIII-4	1604	Malabar			
30	Mardin 18 (incomplete)	1605		X	4	
31	Rome, Vat. Syr. 303, fos. 23^v–27^v	1608	Alqosh	Y	22	
32	Jerusalem 22	1655			23	
33	Qasha Khoshawa Ritual, Q.3, fo. 9^r–Q.4, fo. 3^v	1664	Webb-B	a	24	
34	Baghdad, CP 280, pp. 38–43	1670	Alqosh		25	b
35	Woodbrooke, Ming. Syr. 53, fos. 19^v–26^r	1681	Alqosh	b	26	
36	Diarbekir Ritual (Mardin-Diarbekir 32.19?)	1683	Alqosh	c		
37	Paris, BN Syr. 283, fos. 34^v–39^v	1684	Alqosh		27	c
38	Mosul 41	1685	Alqosh	d		
39	Cambridge Add. 2045, 24^r–27^v	1686	Alqosh	e	28	
40	Rome, Vat. Syr. 491	1686	Chaldaean	f		
41	Berlin Or. Quart. 1160 (Assfalg 29), pp. 606–8	1686	Ḥudra			
42	Paris, BN Syr. 89	1689	Malabar		29	

				Macomber	Webb	Spinks
43	Cambridge Oo 1.15, fos. 7^r–9^r (incomplete)	1691	Chaldaean	g	30	
44	Rome, Vat. Syr. 44, fos. 23^v–27^v	1691	Chaldaean	h	31	
45	Paris, BN Syr. 95	1697	Chaldaean		32	
46	Baghdad, CP 38, pp. 58–66	1697	Alqosh	i	33	
47	Paris, BN Syr. 90, fos. 17^r–21^v	1698	Malabar		34	i
48	Paris, BN Syr. 96, pp. 10–19	1699	Chaldaean		35	f
49	Paris, BN Syr. 97	1699	Chaldaean		36	
50	Berlin 40 (Sachau 64), fos. 10^v–15^r	17/18th c.	Alqosh	j	37	
51	Rome, Vat. Borg. Syr. 36	17/18th c.	Malabar	k		
52	Paris, BN Syr. 98	17/18th c.	Chaldaean			
53	Harvard Syr. MS. 12	17/18th c.	Ḥudra			
54	Paris, BN Syr. 88	18th c.	Chaldaean		38	l
55	Paris, BN Syr. 93	18th c.	Chaldaean		39	
56	Oxford, Bodley Ouseley 267, pp. 62–85	18th c.	Chaldaean		40	g
57	Paris, BN Syr. 91	18th c.	Malabar		41	
58	Paris, BN Syr. 92	18th c.	Malabar		42	
59	Baghdad, CP 177, pp. 18–30	18th c.	Chaldaean		44	
60	Mardin Ritual	18th c.	Chaldaean	q		
61	Mardin Ritual	18th c.	Chaldaean	r		
62	Rome, Vat. Syr. 43, fos. 26^r–28^v	1701	Chaldaean	l	45	
63	Baghdad, CP 170	1706	Chaldaean	m		
64	Cambridge Add. 1984, 34^v–38^r	1707	Alqosh		46	d
65	Baghdad, CP 39	1708	Alqosh	n		

				Macomber	Webb	Spinks
66	Paris, BN Syr. 99	1711	Chaldaean		47	
67	Mardin Ritual (Mardin-Diarbekir 33.18?)	1715	Chaldaean	o		
68	Leiden Or. 1215, fos. 64^r–67^r	pre-1720	Malabar		48	k
69	Baghdad, CP 37, fos. 25^r–29^r	1726	Alqosh	p	49	
70	London, BL Add. 25, 874, fos. 12^v–19^r	1740	Chaldaean		50	
71	Rome, Vat. Syr. 290, fos. 9^r–10^v	pre-1751	Malabar		51	j
72	Mardin 31	1753	Alqosh	s		
73	Berlin 42 (Or. Quart. 546), fos. 27^r–32^v	1756	Alqosh	t	52	
74	Rome, Vat. Syr. 291, fos. 18^r–20^r	1766	Chaldaean		53	h
75	Paris, BN Syr. 310, fos. 21^r–31^v	1774	Alqosh		54	e
76	N.–D. des Semences 95	1795				
77	Cambridge Add. 2046A, fos. 28^r–31^v (incomplete)	18/19th c.	Alqosh	u	55	
78	Oxford, Bodley MS Syriac c.10 fos. 12^r–16^r	19th c.				
79	Baghdad, CP 42, fos. 59^v–64^r	1809	Alqosh	v	43	
80	N.–D. des Semences 96	1826				
81	Berlin 41 (Or. Quart. 565), pp. 37–42	1834	Webb-B	w	56	

				Macomber	Webb	Spinks
82	Baghdad, CP 221	1839	Chaldaean	x		
83	Mosul, Mar Ya'qob 6	1850	Chaldaean	y		
84	London, BL Or. 4061, fos. 27^v–38^r	1851	Chaldaean		57	
85	McHardy Codex A, pp. 30–8	1908				
86	McHardy Codex B, pp. 107–14	1908		z		

In the preparation of this edition the following MSS have been collated:

- (a) by autopsy: 4, 8, 14, 19, 25, 28, 35, 39, 43, 56, 64, 70, 77–8, 84–6;
- (b) from microfilm or photocopy: 11–12, 15–16, 41, 59, 62, 68, 74;
- (c) from the transcripts in the Webb Archive: 1–3, 5–7, 9–10, 17, 22–4, 27, 31, 33–4, 37, 44, 46–8, 50, 69, 71, 73, 75, 79, 81.

Some readings were also collated from the transcript of 54 in the Webb Archive, which also contained a collation of 55 against 48, from which some readings were derived, but no complete collation of 54 or 55 was possible.

Data concerning the following MSS are derived entirely from the apparatus in Macomber (1966): 13, 18, 20–1, 30, 36, 38, 40, 51, 60–1, 63, 65, 67, 72, 82–3. It has not been possible to make any use of the following: 26, 29, 32, 42, 45, 49, 52–3, 57–8, 66, 76, 80.

Seven of the MSS collated for this edition were not included in the apparatus of either Macomber (1966) or Spinks (1980): 11, 41, 59, 70, 78, 84–5.

The five categories into which most of the MSS are classified must now be examined more closely. Only one category is distinguished by a formal classification, that of the Ḥudra MSS, i.e. those containing the material proper to the seasons of the liturgical year as distinct from missals or priests' rituals. The Anaphora of Addai and Mari belongs in this connection to the rites of the Easter Vigil, and in some of the older Ḥudra MSS the text of the anaphora is written out, even though some of the common forms are indicated only by an *incipit*. The ten MSS in this category (1–3, 7–8, 11, 13, 15, 41, 53) include the oldest extant texts of this anaphora, and thus constitute a most important witness to the earliest form of the text available to us.

These MSS do not present a homogeneous text. In several passages they are fairly evenly divided between two, or even three, readings. Examples may be found in l. $55^{1°}$, where four (1, 11, 13, 15) have the shorter and five (2, 3, 7, 8, 41) the fuller text, and in l. 48 where four (1, 2, 11, 13) have the shorter text while two (3, 7) have the additional word in the earlier and three (8, 15, 41) in the later position. Six readings may nevertheless be described as characteristic of the group, in that never more than two MSS diverge from the rest, although only one of these readings (that in l. 11) is common to the whole group, and only one (that in l. 16) is exclusive to the group. The six readings in question are the shorter readings in ll. 10, 11, $16^{2°}$, $46^{1°}$ and $55^{2°}$ and the reading ܪܟܘܣܐ without a suffix in l. 40. It may be noted that MS 8 diverges from the group in one, MS 11 in at least two, and MS 41 in three of these six readings. More generally it may be noted that MS 7 is the only one never to diverge from a reading common to most of the group, while MSS 8 and 11 each diverge five times and MS 41 three times in company with one or two other Hudra MSS, and MSS 11 and 41 have respectively three and five independent readings as well.

Webb (1967–8) divides the MSS that do not belong to the Ḥudra group or to either the Chaldaean or the Malabar traditions into two categories which he designates Groups A and B. Group A is essentially identical with Macomber's Alqosh tradition, while Group B is not classified separately by Macomber, although he does comment on the two latest MSS in this group. He notes that MS 81 'seems to have been copied from a much older ritual and preserves many archaic readings', while MS 33 also stands rather apart from the categories into which most MSS later than the mid-seventeenth century fall (Macomber, 1966, p. 356). Webb's Group B consists of nine MSS (4, 9, 10, 12, 16, 17, 24, 33, 81). The distinctive characteristic readings on which Webb based his classification fall mostly outside the anaphora itself, but the reading ܡܪܒܝܢܘܬܗ with suffix in l. 60 is found in all but two of the Group B MSS (the exceptions being MSS 10 and 17) as well as in six of the Ḥudra MSS and those of the Chaldaean tradition. Two other readings that may be regarded as characteristic, though not exclusively so, of the

Group B MSS are the shorter reading in l. 11 (in agreement with the Ḥudra MSS, although MSS 16 and 81 diverge here from the rest of Group B) and the fuller reading in l. $14^{1°}$ (in agreement with three Ḥudra MSS (8, 11, 41) as well as with those of the Alqosh and Malabar traditions). The agreement of the Group B MSS with some or all of the Ḥudra MSS in each of these characteristic readings suggests that they too are important witnesses to the earliest extant form of the text. It is significant that two of these readings are found also in MS 6 and all three in MSS 5 and 86.

In three passages (ll. $16^{1°}$, $55^{2°}$, and $56^{2°}$) the MSS in Group B are fairly evenly divided between two readings, and in l. 40 they are divided between three readings: three (4, 17, 18) read ܟ̇ܣܘܬܐ without any suffix, four (9, 10, 12, 16) add a second-masculine-singular suffix, and two (24, 33) add a third-masculine-singular suffix. In general it may be noted that three of the group diverge from the rest in two passages (9, 10, 12 in l. $46^{1°}$ and 9, 12, 81 in l. 48), and two diverge from all or all but one of the rest in nine passages. Within these minority readings two pairings occur twice each: MSS 9 and 12 in the two passages just mentioned, each time with a different third partner, and MSS 4 and 9 in ll. $51^{2°}$ and $59^{1°}$. One pairing, that of MSS 10 and 17, occurs five times: in l. 60 (see above), in ll. 23 and 54, and in the two readings characteristic of MSS of the Malabar tradition in ll. $50^{1°}$ and $53^{3°}$. In ten passages one of the group has a distinctive reading, the highest occurrences being in MSS 16 and 81, with four and three respectively. The distinctive shared reading of MSS 9, 10, 12 in l. $46^{1°}$ is found also in nearly all the Ḥudra MSS. Any reading with substantial attestation in both Ḥudra and Group B MSS must be considered very seriously.

Most of the later MSS fall into three categories, of which the most important is the Alqosh tradition, which is that of the East Syrian Church itself and has remained free from Roman influence. Eleven MSS were assigned to this tradition by both Macomber and Webb, and each added to the category further MSS not included in the other's list. The only discrepancy arises over MSS 23 and 27, which were unclassified by Macomber, but placed in this category by Webb. The characteristics used by Webb in determining this category again fall outside the anaphora itself. Within the text of the anaphora there are no readings exclusively characteristic of this group, although there are six readings (to be found in ll. $14^{1°}$, $16^{1°}$ 40, $46^{1°}$, 54, and 60) in which most of the Alqosh MSS agree. All of these readings, however, are found also in the MSS of the Malabar tradition, and three of them (those in ll. 16, 40, and 46) also in those of the Chaldaean tradition. The fact that MSS 23 and 27 each share all these six readings vindicates Webb's inclusion of them in this group. It is also of interest that MSS 27 and 50 share two of the readings characteristic of some or all of the oldest MSS (those in ll. 11 and 55$^{1°}$. The twenty-two MSS assigned to the Alqosh tradition are the following: 19–20, 22–3, 27, 31, 34–9, 46, 50, 64–5, 69, 72–3, 75, 77, 79.

To the Chaldaean tradition, reflecting in some degree the influence of the 'union' with Rome in 1552, Macomber and Webb between them assign a further twenty-two MSS: 40, 43–5, 48–9, 52, 54–6, 59–63, 66–7, 70, 74, 82–4. Within the text of the anaphora eight readings may be said to be characteristic of this tradition, of which three are fairly distinctive: the shorter text in ll. 26 and 46$^{2°}$ and the third-masculine-singular suffix in ܘܡܩܒܠܗ in l. 59. It is interesting that all three of these readings are found also in MS 16, constituting three of the four passages in which that MS has a reading distinct from that of the rest of the Group B MSS. The other five readings characteristic of the Chaldaean tradition are to be found also in ll. 16$^{1°}$, 40, 46$^{1°}$, 54, and 60, the first three being common also to the Alqosh and Malabar traditions. A further reading found exclusively in Chaldaean MSS, though with certainty in only ten and with certainty not in a further six, is the longer reading in l. 38.

To the Malabar tradition Macomber and Webb assign nine MSS: 25, 29, 42, 47, 51, 57–8, 68, 71). In addition to the six characteristic readings shared between the Alqosh and Malabar traditions already listed there are two that are fairly distinctive of the Malabar tradition, though both are found also in two of the Group B MSS (10 and 17; see above) and two of the unclassified MSS (14 and 18); the first is found also in MSS 6 and 21. The two readings in question are the addition of ܘܡܚܣܐ to ܣܚܝ in l. 50 and the omission of ܘܡܚܣܝܢ in l. 53.

The absence for the most part of readings distinctively characteristic of each of the five categories of MSS makes it difficult on the basis of the text of the anaphora alone to categorize the remaining fourteen. No attempt at classification is possible in the case of the four (26, 32, 76, 80) that have not been collated at all. In the case of three (18, 21, 30) our knowledge is confined to the data in Macomber's apparatus. In the case of MS 18 we have noted its agreement with

MSS 10 and 17 and those of the Malabar tradition in ll. 50 and 53, and there is nothing we can add to this. In the case of MS 21 we have noted that it shares at least the essential element of the reading in l. 50 (with two Hudra MSS), but not the one in l. 53; it also shares the Hudra readings in ll. 40 and 55[2°]. At l. 14[1°] it agrees with five of the Hudra MSS and those of the Chaldaean tradition against the reading of the B group and the other unclassified MSS, while at l. 59[2°] it agrees again with the Chaldaean MSS in company with MS 16. Of MS 30 nothing can be said.

Of the remaining seven unclassified MSS, MS 14 is extant only from l. 43. Its agreement with MSS 10 and 17 and the Malabar MSS in ll. 50 and 53 has already been noted; its other significant agreement is with the Hudra MSS in l. 46[1°], where it is joined by MSS 5 and 6 and three of the Group B MSS (9, 10, 12). MSS 5, 6, and 86 each have several agreements with the Hudra MSS: in addition to the reading in l. 46[1°] just mentioned in MSS 5 and 6, all three of these share the Hudra readings in ll. 11 and 40, and MS 6 shares that in l. 55[2°] too. In l. 60 MSS 5 and 86 agree with six Hudra MSS, seven in Group B, and most of the Chaldaean MSS. In l. 54 MS 5 agrees with two Hudra MSS, six in Group B, and most of the Chaldaean MSS in reading the shorter form of the addition. In l. 56[2°] MSS 6 and 86 agree with four Group B MSS (4, 12, 24, 33) in the fuller reading. MS 6 further agrees with the Malabar reading in l. 50 already mentioned, and with four Hudra MSS (1, 11, 13, 15) and one in Group B (81) in the shorter reading in l. 55[1°]. MSS 6 and 85 agree with six Hudra MSS and four in Group B in omitting the *waw* in l. 16[1°]. MSS 78 and 85 both contain Institution Narratives (after ll. 23 and 30 respectively), which suggests Chaldaean affiliation, but neither of them has any of the distinctively Chaldaean readings in ll. 26, 38, 46, and 59. At l. 56[1°] MS 78 omits the *waw* in company with one Hudra MS (1) and two Group B MSS (24 and 33).

MS 28 requires separate consideration, since its fo. 17 is a supplementary text. This folio contains the text from the last word of l. 43 to the middle of l. 60, and it is probable that the supplement represents a different tradition from that of the rest of the MS. Although fo. 17 ends with the word ܟܕܩܘܒܠܗ with the suffix, the reading found in six Hudra MSS, seven in Group B, MSS 5 and 86, and most of the Chaldaean MSS, fo. 18 begins with ܐܬܪ ܐܚܘܫܒܗ, which led Webb (Spinks, 1980, p. 22) rightly to suspect that the original reading of MS 28 was ܪܝܢ ܪܚܘܬܒܪܢ as in the MSS of the Alqosh and Malabar traditions.

MS 28 itself (i.e. in ll. 1–43 and 61–end) has further agreements with the Alqosh and Malabar MSS at ll. $14^{1°}$, $16^{1°}$, and 40, although the first of these is shared with those in Group B and the other two with the Chaldaean MSS. There are no agreements with any of the four characteristic Ḥudra readings or with either of the two distinctively characteristic Chaldaean readings that are found in these parts of the text. It seems reasonable to conclude that the closest affinities of the original MS 28 are with the tradition common to the Alqosh and Malabar MSS.

The text of the supplement (designated MS 28^a), as we have seen, shares the reading of six Ḥudra MSS, seven in Group B, and MSS 5 and 86 in l. 60. It shares neither of the distinctively Malabar readings and neither of the distinctively Chaldaean readings found in this part of the text. In l. $46^{1°}$ it shares the reading of six Group B MSS and those of the Alqosh, Chaldaean, and Malabar traditions as well as four other of the unclassified MSS (21, 78, 85, 86). In l. 54 it shares the shorter form of the addition with two Ḥudra MSS, six in Group B, and MS 5, as well as most of the Chaldaean MSS. In l. $55^{2°}$ it shares the reading of most of the Ḥudra MSS, four in Group B, and MSS 6 and 21. In l. $56^{2°}$ it shares the reading of four Group B MSS and MSS 6 and 86. Its closest affinities seem therefore to be with the Ḥudra and Group B MSS, and it is reasonable to conclude that the exemplar from which the supplement was made had a much older and better text than that of the exemplar of the main MS.

Looking back over the unclassified MSS as a group, we may conclude that while none of them can clearly be placed in any one of the five categories, most of them contain a number of significant agreements with Ḥudra and Group B MSS. This is particularly true of MSS 5, 6, 14, 21, 28^a, and 86. Where these agree with Ḥudra MSS or those of Group B, they constitute a significant witness to the older forms of the text.

Readings attested in only one MS are most unlikely to represent the original text, although in two passages a unique reading of MS 1 has been adopted in the eclectic text below: ll. $14^{2°}$ and $50^{1°}$; in the latter passage it is the original reading of MS 1 that has been adopted. The chief importance otherwise of such singular readings is as an indication of the quality of the MS in which they are found. Readings that occur in only two MSS are sometimes worthy of consideration; a few appear in the apparatus. A series of such exclusive agreements, such as those already mentioned between MSS 10 and 17, may indicate a relationship between those particular MSS. In a text of this length, however, it is hardly to be expected that sufficient evidence by way of common omissions and erroneous readings will arise as to establish direct dependence in the sense that one of the pair is the exemplar from which the other was copied. Agreements may sometimes be accidental. The idiomatic phrase ܪܒܐ ܪܒܘܬܐ ܒܥ ('dealt very graciously'), for instance, occurs twice in this text, in ll. 13 and 23. The word ܪܒܐ (literally 'great') is omitted in l. 13 by MSS 3 and 10 and in l. 23 by MSS 2, 10, and 17. It is most unlikely that MS 10 represents a sole consistent survival of an older form of the idiom without the adjective, and there is nothing in this instance to suggest a relationship between these MSS, since MS 10 is the only one to omit the adjective in both passages, and its companions are different in the two cases. By far the most likely explanation is independent occurrence of the same error.

It is unnecessary to give a complete account of all the singular readings or those attested by only a few MSS. But it may be useful to append notes on the unusual readings of some of the more significant MSS in order to facilitate an evaluation of their character.

1 Mar Esh'aya Ḥudra

It is unnecessary to print singular readings of this MS since they can be found readily in Macomber (1966). It is sufficient to note that they may be found at ll. 8, 15, 36, (1*), 37, 43 and 52(1ª). The third of these probably, and the last two certainly, are erroneous, while one of the others is an omission of initial *waw* ('and'), and the first is simply the improbable substitution of the emphatic for the absolute state.

2 Diarbekir Ḥudra (Mardin-Diarbekir 31. 47)

Three errors may be noted in this MS: the omission of *rish* in the last word in l. 23 and of *dalath* in the first word of l. 24, and the passive form of the two verbs at the beginning of l. 57. In the light of this, little weight attaches to its other singular readings: the substitution of ܪܘܚܢܐ ('of spiritual beings') for ܫܡܝ̈ܢܐ ('of heavenly beings') in l. 14, the omission of the suffix to ܢܕܥܘܢܟ ('that . . . may know *thee*') in l. 43, involving a departure from the biblical source in John 17: 3, and the substitution of ܛܘܦܣܐ ܘܡܫܠܡܢܘܬܐ ('the example and tradition') for ܒܡܫܠܡܢܘܬܐ ܛܘܦܣܐ ('by tradition the example') in l. 52.

3 Mardin 22

This MS has fewer *incipit*s than most early MSS, and is particularly valuable for its complete text of the first part of the *Sanctus*. On the other hand its usefulness is marred by a number of errors: the substitution of *caph* for *lamadh* in the last word in l. 31, of *rish* for *dalath*, together with omission of the following *'e*, in the first word in l. 43, the omission of the second *yudh* in the penultimate word in l. 51, the passive form of the first verb in l. 57, and the substitution of a second- for the third-masculine-singular suffix in the third word in l. 62. It has no other singular readings.

4 Cambridge Add. 2046B

The omission of the plural ending (*waw*) of the verb in l. 50 (also in MSS 16 and 56) is to be regarded as an orthographic variant. The omission of the second and third words of l. 15 is probably a semi-mechanical error, although the resultant text is intelligible. For the other singular reading of this MS see the textual note on l. 40.

5 Diarbekir 48

The omission of the third word in l. 37 is an error, since the *waw* is retained at the beginning of the following word. The prefixing of *waw* to l. 22 is also an error, since it duplicates the *waw* at the beginning of the previous line. The only other singular reading of this MS is the addition of ܡܪܝܡܐ ('Most High') after the second word in l. 7.

6 Mardin 19

For the only singular reading of this MS see the textual note on l. 48.

7 Baghdad, CP 333

The inversion ܐܝܬ ܠܗܘܢ in l. 54 is most improbable. Macomber attributes it to MS 10, but it occurs in Webb's transcript of MS 7. The omission of the last word of l. 60 (found also in MS 79) is unlikely to reflect an ancient reading.

8 London, BL Or. 5750

This MS begins at l. 8. Two errors of the original copyist are the omissions of *dalath* in the second word in l. 48 and of *lamadh* in the first word in l. 58. Two more substantial omissions are those of the last three words of l. 16 and the last two words of l. 38.

9 Berlin 38

For the only singular reading in this MS see the textual notes on l. 56.

10 Baghdad, CP 36

There are no readings peculiar to this MS.

11 Berlin 47

This MS does not contain the text of ll. 1–9. Much of the contents of ll. 27–30 and 54–6 has perished. The writing is untidy and gives the impression of carelessness. Apart from errors apparently corrected *calamo currente* in ll. 53 and 62, the omission of the initial *dalath* in the third word of l. 49, of the *shin* in the last word of l. 62, and of the whole of the first word of l. 54, together with the repetition by dittography of the third word in l. 62, are certainly errors, and the omission of the *waw* at the beginning of l. 60 is probably also to be reckoned an error. In the light of this no significance is to be attached to the two remaining singular readings of this MS, the insertion of ܡܪܝ ('O my Lord') after the first words of ll. 43 and 63.

12 Rouen Or. 21

The only singular reading of this MS is the insertion of ܢܩܕܘܬܐ ܘ ('the temperance and') before ܕܟܝܘܬܐ ('the purity') in l. 47.

15 Rome, Vat. Borg. Syr. 150

This MS has a maximum of abbreviations with mere *incipit*s, and does not contain the text of ll. 1–9. It omits the pronoun ܐܢܬ in l. 40, attaching the *dalath* immediately to the verb. For its other singular reading see the textual notes on l. 50.

16 Rome, Vat. Syr. 66

Two omissions of the original copyist (those of the third word in l. 38 and the fifth word in l. 45) are to be regarded as erroneous. For the singular readings of this MS see the textual notes on ll. 13 and 56. The supplementary fo. 101a is a secondary insertion of an Institution Narrative.

17 Alqosh 70

This MS contains one error at the beginning of l. 51, where the final *nun* of the pronoun is replaced by an *'alaph*. The only singular reading, the omission of the last two words in l. 61, is hardly likely to be ancient.

19 London, BL Add. 7181

There is a lacuna in this MS between fos. 36 and 37, resulting in the loss of ll. 36–54.

22 Baghdad, CP 40

Probably no significance is to be attached to the omission of ll. 5 and 6. The omission of *waw* at the beginning of l. 29 (also in MS 47) can hardly be other than accidental in a series of clauses so related.

23 Baghdad, CP 209

This MS lacks the beginning of the text (as far as the third word in l. 12). The apparent inversion of the fourth and fifth words in l. 23 must be an error, and the substitution of *waw* for *dalath* at the beginning of the third word in l. 57 is probably also an error. These two letters are not infrequently confused in biblical MSS. The only singular reading of this MS, the omission of the sixth word in l. 14, is probably also to be regarded as an error.

24 Berlin 39

The omission of l. 15 and the first two words of l. 16 is probably a semi-mechanical error, while the omission of *dalath* in the first word of l. 49 and the substitution of *dalath* for *waw* at the beginning of the third word in l. 61 are also to be regarded as errors.

28 Manchester, Rylands Syr. 19

In addition to an error corrected *calamo currente* in l. 48, there are two uncorrected errors in this MS: the omission of *seyāmē* on the last word in l. 13, and the substitution of *rish* for *dalath* in the second word in l. 45.

41 Berlin Or. Quart. 1160

This MS does not contain ll. 1–9, for which it refers to the Anaphora of Theodore. Two errors have been noted: the insertion of ܐܬ̈ܡܘܝ ('days') before ܝܪܘܡܥ ('the inhabitants') in l. 43, and the omission of the *waw* at the beginning of the last word in l. 53. At l. 21 ܐܝܢܝܡܫ ('heavenly') is recorded in the margin in a different hand as an alternative reading to ܐܟ̈ܠܐܡܕ ('of angels') which replaces it in the text. At l. 38 it omits ܐܢ̈ܐܟ̇ܘ ('and just'). At l. 51 it adds ܐܝ̈ܛܚܘ ('and sinful') after ܐܠܝ̈ܚܡ ('frail'), thus departing from the formula common to ll. 22 and 51. It omits the whole of l. 63. For other singular readings of this MS see the textual notes on ll. 14 and 15. It is notable for the relatively high number of singular readings.

81 Berlin 41

For singular readings of this MS see the textual notes on ll. 59 and 60.

Note on the Text

THE text printed below is an eclectic text. It has emerged from a critical sifting of the oldest and best MS evidence at present available. The critical apparatus has been restricted to variant readings that are thought to have a serious claim to originality, other readings (including singular readings of the oldest MSS and readings found only in later MSS) being relegated either to the textual notes which follow the text or to the notes on individual MSS. The apparatus contains readings found in thirty-two MSS, 1–24 in the list above, supplemented by the following eight: 28, 30, 33, 41, 78, 81, 85–6. The principles of selection have been to include first all the oldest MSS (to c.1600), then the remaining Hudra (41) and Group B (33 and 81) ones, and finally the remaining MSS which do not clearly belong to any of the five categories (28, 30, 78, 85, and 86). This selection includes the four oldest MSS of the Alqosh tradition (19, 20, 22, and 23), but none of those of the Chaldaean or Malabar traditions, it being thought unlikely that any readings found exclusively in these traditions are ancient.

The extent of the material included in the anaphora varies slightly in different editions. The present text begins with the celebrant's greeting 'The grace . . .', which is the point at which Syrian anaphoras usually begin, and the earlier material in ll. 1–14 in Macomber (1966) is not included here. Within the text it may be noted that ll. 4, 9, 34, 35, and 67 are omitted in some MSS; in some cases they may be implicit in material indicated only by an *incipit*. Such abbreviations and omissions have not been noted in the apparatus. Two more complex cases are discussed in the textual notes on ll. 42 and 56.

At this point it will be useful to give some indication of what is not included in this edition. In the first place no account has been taken of printed editions of the text; we are concerned here solely with the evidence of the MSS. In the second place rubrical material has been excluded, in particular that concerning the repetition of certain phrases, which adds nothing to the actual content of the text. The assignment of material to the priest, deacon, and congregation has been indicated for convenience, but is not part of the critical text, and no notice has been made of occasional variations such as the assignment of the final *Amen* to the deacon instead of to the congregation in MS 70. Common forms such as the *Sanctus* and the doxologies, which are often indicated only by an *incipit* (as in the Mar Esh'aya Hudra), are on the other hand printed out in full according to what seem to be the oldest traditional forms. The evidence for these is given in the textual notes. No record is made of the abbreviation of certain words in some MSS; in no case does this give rise to any doubt as to the reading. Nor is any record made of purely orthographic variants or of cases of *adiunctio* and *disiunctio*.

The view has been taken that the *Cushapha* ('whispering') prayers, although doubtless stemming from a long tradition (cf. Spinks, 1982–3) are not authentic elements of the anaphora itself, which is couched consistently in the first-person plural, except for occasional addresses to the deity in the form ‏,ܝܡ‎, 'O my Lord'. Finally no reference is made in the apparatus to readings of the Maronite anaphora *Sharar*; the relationship between this anaphora and that of Addai and Mari is regarded as a matter for literary rather than textual criticism.

The terms *omnes* and *ceteri* in the critical apparatus refer to those of the thirty-two MSS whose readings are included in the apparatus that are extant for the reading in question, but they do not necessarily include MSS 13, 18, 20–21, and 30 unless their reading is clear from the apparatus in Macomber (1966). MSS listed after *minus* are indicated as reading the text rather than the variant.

Occasional discrepancies between the material presented here and that in the apparatus of Macomber (1966) and Spinks (1980) arise in cases where the present editor has not had access to original MSS, but has been dependent on the transcripts in the Webb Archive. The only one of any importance is in l. 51, where the uncertainty as to the reading of MS 3 is due to the fact that Webb's transcript includes the additional words, while Macomber's apparatus lists this among the MSS that do not contain them. Such a discrepancy can be resolved only by recourse to the MS itself. Macomber's apparatus is inaccurate in at least one detail: the reading ‏ܪܚܡܘܗܝ‎ which he attributes to MS 4 in l. 47 is definitely not that of the MS, which has the usual reading, ‏ܪܚܡܘܗܝ‎. Comparison of the apparatus in Macomber (1966) and Spinks (1980) reveals some inaccuracies in the latter in material taken over from the former. There are some further inaccuracies in the additional material in Spinks's apparatus provided by Webb, but none of these is serious.

The text is accompanied by a translation which has been freshly made for this edition. It is couched in traditional language, and is for the most part as literal as possible; where idiomatic considerations have dictated a non-literal rendering, this is indicated in the Commentary. The variants in the critical apparatus are not separately translated here, but the difference in meaning is clearly indicated in the textual notes. Spinks's useful division of the text into nine sections, A–I, has been adopted in both the text and the translation.

ܩܘܕܫܐ ܕܫܠܝ̈ܚܐ

The Sanctification of the Apostles

A

1 P ܠܫܘܒܚܗ ܕܡܪܢ ܝܫܘܥ ܡܫܝܚܐ. ܘܫܘܒܚܗ ܕܐܠܗܐ ܐܒܐ.

2 ܘܫܘܬܦܘܬܐ ܕܪܘܚܐ ܕܩܘܕܫܐ. ܬܗܘܐ ܥܡ ܟܠܢ.
3 ܗܫܐ ܘܒܟܠܙܒܢ ܘܠܥܠܡ ܥܠܡܝܢ.
4 R ܐܡܝܢ.
5 P ܠܟܠ ܢܗܘܘܢ ܡܕܒ̈ܚܘܢ.
6 R ܠܘܬܟ ܐܠܗܗ ܕܐܒܪܗܡ ܘܕܐܝܣܚܩ ܘܕܝܣܪܝܠ. ܡܠܟܐ ܡܫܝܚܐ.
7 P ܘܩܘܪܒܢܐ ܠܐܠܗܐ ܡܪ ܟܠ ܡܬܩܪܒ.
8 R ܫܘܐ ܘܙܕܩ.
9 D ܫܠܡܐ ܥܡܟ.

B

10 P ܫܘܐ ܠܬܫܒܘܚܐ ܡܢ ܟܠ ܦܘ̈ܡܝܢ. ܘܬܘܕܝܬܐ ܡܢ ܟܠ ܠܫ̈ܢܝܢ.

11 ܫܡܐ ܣܓܝܐܐ ܘܡܫܒܚܐ ܕܐܒܐ ܘܒܪܐ ܘܪܘܚܐ ܕܩܘܕܫܐ.

12 ܕܒܪܐ ܥܠܡܐ ܒܛܝܒܘܬܗ. ܘܒܚܢܢܗ، ܒܡܪܚܡܢܘܬܗ.

13 ܘܦܪܩ ܒܢܝ̈ܢܫܐ ܒܚܢܢܗ. ܘܒܗ̇ ܛܝܒܘܬܐ ܪܒܬܐ ܠܘܬ ܡܝ̈ܘܬܐ.

C

14 ܠܡܪܘܬܟ ܡܪܝ، ܣܓܕܝܢ ܐܦ ܐ̈ܠܦܝܢ ܕܡܠܐܟܐ ܘܪܒܘ ܪ̈ܒܘܢ ܕܥܝ̈ܪܐ.
15 ܘܡܫܪ̈ܝܬܐ ܕܪ̈ܘܚܢܐ. ܡܫ̈ܡܫܢܐ ܕܢܘܪܐ ܘܕܪܘܚܐ. ܠܫܡܟ ܡܩܕܫܝܢ.
16 ܥܡ ܒܘܪ̈ܟܐ ܘܣܓܕ̈ܬܐ ܡܫ̈ܒܚܬܐ. ܟܕ ܩܥܝܢ ܘܡܩܕܫܝܢ ܕܠܐ ܫܠܝܐ.

14 ܣܓܕܝܢ] *pr.* ܘ ܒܪܟܝܢ B + 5–6, 8, 11, 19, 22–3, 28, 41, 78, 85–6 ܕܥܝ̈ܪܐ] *add.* ܡܩ̈ܕܫܝܢ 3, 6, 8, 15, 41; *add.* ܡܫ̈ܒܚܐ *ceteri minus* 1 **15** ܡܫ̈ܡܫܢܐ] *pr. waw* 3, 6, 8, 11, 21–3 **16** ܥܡ] pr. waw 5, 10–11, 15–17, 19, 23, 28, 33, 78, 86 ܘܣܓܕ̈ܬܐ ܡܫ̈ܒܚܐ] *tr. et add.* ܪ̈ܘܚܢܐ *omnes minus* 1–3, 7–8, 15, 41; *add.* ܣܓܕ̈ܬܐ ܠܡܪܘܬܟ ܡܝܩܪܝܢ 4–6, 10, 16–17, 19, 22–4, 28, 33, 41, 78, 81, 85–6

A

1	*Priest*	The grace of our Lord Jesus Christ and the love of God the Father
2		and the fellowship of the Holy Spirit be with us all,
3		now and at all times and for ever and ever.
4	*Response*	Amen.
5	*Priest*	Let your hearts be on high.
6	*Response*	To thee, the God of Abraham and of Isaac and of Israel, the glorious King.
7	*Priest*	The offering is being offered to God the Lord of all.
8	*Response*	It is meet and right.
9	*Deacon*	Peace be with us.

B

10	*Priest*	Worthy of praise from every mouth and thanksgiving from every tongue
11		is the adorable and glorious name of the Father and the Son and the Holy Spirit,
12		who created the world in his grace and its inhabitants in his loving-kindness,
13		and redeemed the sons of men in his mercy, and dealt very graciously with mortals.

C

14		Thy majesty, O my Lord, a thousand thousand heavenly beings and myriad myriads of angels adore
15		and the hosts of spiritual beings, the ministers of fire and of spirit, glorifying thy name
16		with the cherubim and the holy seraphim, ceaselessly crying out and glorifying

17 ܘܦܩܝ ܗܢܐ ܠܗܢܐ ܘܐܡܪܝ.
18 R ܩܕܝܫ ܩܕܝܫ ܩܕܝܫ ܡܪܝܐ ܚܝܠܬܢܐ. ܕܡܠܝܢ ܫܡܝܐ ܘܐܪܥܐ
ܡܢ ܬܫܒܘܚܬܗ.
19 [ܐܘܫܥܢܐ ܒܡܪܘܡܐ. ܐܘܫܥܢܐ ܠܒܪܗ ܕܕܘܝܕ..
20 ܒܪܝܟ ܕܐܬܐ ܘܐܬܐ ܒܫܡܗ ܕܡܪܝܐ. ܐܘܫܥܢܐ ܒܡܪܘܡܐ.]

D

21 P ܘܥܡ ܗܠܝܢ ܚܝܠ̈ܘܬܐ ܫܡܝ̈ܢܝܐ ܡܘܕܝܢ ܠܟ ܡܪܝ،

22 ܐܦ ܚܢ ܥܒ̈ܕܝܟ ܡܚܝ̈ܠܐ ܘܡܟܝܟܐ ܘܕܘܝܐ.
23 ܕܥܒܕܬ ܥܡܢ ܛܝܒܘܬܐ ܪܒܬܐ ܕܠܐ ܡܬܦܪܥܐ.

24 ܒܕܠܒܫܬ ܐܢܫܘܬܢ ܕܬܚܝܢ ܒܐܠܗܘܬܟ.

25 ܘܪܡܪܡܬ ܫܦܠܢ. ܘܐܩܝܡܬ ܡܦܘܠܬܢ.
26 ܘܚܝܬ ܡܝܘܬܘܬܢ. ܘܫܒܩܬ ܚܘ̈ܒܝܢ.
27 ܘܙܕܩܬ ܠܚܛܝܘܬܢ. ܘܐܢܗܪܬ ܠܝܕܥܬܢ.

28 ܘܚܝܒܬ ܡܪܢ ܘܐܠܗܢ ܠܒܥܠܕܒ̈ܒܝܢ.
29 ܘܙܟܝܬ ܠܟܝܢܘܬܗ ܕܟܝܢܢ ܚܠܫܐ.
30 ܒܪ̈ܚܡܐ ܥܬܝܪ̈ܐ ܕܛܝܒܘܬܟ.
31 ܘܥܠ ܐܦ̈ ܟܠܗܘܢ ܥܘܕܪ̈ܢܝܟ ܘܛܝܒܘܬܟ ܕܠܘܬܢ.
32 ܢܣܩ ܠܟ ܬܫܒܘܚܬܐ ܘܐܝܩܪܐ ܘܬܘܕܝܬܐ ܘܣܓܕܬܐ.

33 ܗܫܐ ܘܒܟܠܙܒܢ ܘܠܥܠܡ ܥܠ̈ܡܝܢ.
34 R ܐܡܝܢ.
35 D ܒܠ̈ܒܘܬܟܘܢ ܨܠܘ. ܫܠܡܐ ܥܡܢ.

E

36 P ܐܢܬ ܡܪܝ، ܒܪ̈ܚܡܝܟ ܣܓܝ̈ܐܐ ܕܠܐ ܡܬܡܠܠܝܢ.
37 ܥܒܕ ܕܘܟܪܢܐ ܛܒܐ ܘܡܩܒܠܐ
38 ܠܟܠܗܘܢ ܐܒܗ̈ܬܐ ܟܐ̈ܢܐ ܘܙܕ̈ܝܩܐ ܕܫܦܪܘ ܩܕܡܝܟ.

39 ܒܕܘܟܪܢܐ ܕܦܓܪܗ ܘܕܡܗ ܕܡܫܝܚܟ.

17 and calling to one another and saying:

18 *Response* Holy, holy, holy is the Lord Almighty: the heavens and the earth are full of his glory.

19 (Hosanna in the highest! Hosanna to the Son of David!

20 Blessed is he who has come and comes in the name of the Lord. Hosanna in the highest!)

D

21 *Priest* And with these heavenly hosts we give thee thanks, O my Lord,

22 we also thy unworthy, frail, and miserable servants,

23 because thou hast dealt very graciously with us in a way which cannot be repaid,

24 in that thou didst assume our humanity that thou mightest restore us to life by thy divinity,

25 and didst exalt our low estate, and raise up our fallen state,

26 and resurrect our mortality, and forgive our sins,

27 and acquit our sinfulness, and enlighten our understanding,

28 and, our Lord and God, overcome our adversaries,

29 and give victory to the unworthiness of our frail nature

30 in the overflowing mercies of thy grace.

31 And for all thy benefits and graces towards us

32 we offer thee glory and honour and thanksgiving and adoration

33 now and at all times and for ever and ever.

34 *Response* Amen.

35 *Deacon* Pray in your hearts. Peace be with us.

E

36 *Priest* Do thou, O my Lord, in thy manifold and ineffable mercies

37 make a good and gracious remembrance

38 for all the upright and just fathers who were pleasing before thee,

39 in the commemoration of the body and blood of thy Christ,

40 ܕܡܩܪܒܝܢ ܠܟ ܟܠ ܡܕܒܚܐ ܕܒܢܝܐ ܘܡܩܕܫܐ.
ܐܝܟܢܐ ܕܐܢܬ ܐܠܗܢ.
41 ܘܒܗܕ. ܒܗܝ ܥܝܢܟ ܘܫܠܡܟ ܠܟܠܗܘܢ ܢܗܘܬܗ ܕܒܠܒܐ.

42 (R ܐܡܝܢ.)

F

43 P ܕܢܕܒܪܢ ܠܟܠܗܘܢ ܒܡܘܪܝܗ ܕܐܪܥܐ.
44 ܕܐܢܬ ܐܢܬ ܐܠܗܐ ܐܒܐ ܕܫܪܪܐ ܒܠܚܘܕܝܟ.
45 ܘܐܢܬ ܫܕܪܬ ܠܒܪܟ ܝܫܘܥ ܡܫܝܚܐ. ܒܪܟ ܘܚܒܝܒܟ.

46 ܘܗܘ ܡܪܢ ܘܐܠܗܢ ܐܠܦ ܠܢ ܒܡܟܪܙܘܬܗ ܡܫܝܚܝܬܐ.

47 ܠܟܠܗ ܕܟܝܢܘܬܐ ܘܩܕܝܫܘܬܐ ܕܢܒ̈ܝܐ ܘܫ̈ܠܝܚܐ
ܘܣ̈ܗܕܐ ܘܡ̈ܠܦܢܐ
48 ܘܐܦܝܣܩܘܦܐ ܘܩܫ̈ܝܫܐ ܘܡ̈ܫܡܫܢܐ.
49 ܘܠܟܠܗܘܢ ܒ̈ܢܝܗ ܕܥܕܬܐ ܩܕܝܫܬܐ ܩܬܘܠܝܩܝ.
50 ܐܝܟ ܕܐܬܪܫܡܘ ܒܦܘܩܕܢܐ ܕܡܫܡܫܢܘܬܐ ܩܕܝܫܬܐ.

G

51 ܘܐܦ ܚܢܢ ܡܪܝ، ܥܒ̈ܕܝܟ ܚܛܝ̈ܐ ܘܡܚܝ̈ܠܐ ܘܕܘܝ̈ܐ.
ܕܡܫܡܫܝܢ ܘܡܫܒܚܝܢ ܠܡܕܒܚܟ.
52 ܘܡܨܠܝܢ ܒܗܝܟܠܐ ܛܘܦܣܐ ܕܡܪܟ.

53 ܟܕ ܫܒܚܝܢ ܘܡܫܒܚܝܢ ܘܡܪܡܪܡܝܢ ܘܡܣܓܕܝܢ.

40 ܡܕܒܚܐ] ܡܕܒܚܝܟ 8–10, 12, 16, 22–3, 28, 41, 78, 85 ܡܕܒܚܗ 24, 33 **44** ܐܒܐ] *om.* 8, 24 **46** ܐܠܦ] *pr.* ܘ ܐܬܐ 4, 16–17, 21–4, 28^{a}, 33, 78, 81, 85–6 **48** ܘܐܦܝܣܩܘܦܐ] *add.* ܘܦ̈ܪܝܕܘܛܐ 4–6, 8, 10, 14–17, 22, 24, 28^{a}, 33, 41, 78, 85–6; *pr.* ܘܦ̈ܪܝܕܘܛܐ 3, 7, 9, 12, 21, 23, 81 **50** ܒܦܘܩܕܢܐ] *add.* ܚܝܐ B + 1^{a}, 3, 5–8, 11, 14, 18, 20, 22–3, 28^{a}, 41, 78, 85–6; *add. praeterea* ܘܡܚܝܢܐ 6, 10, 14, 17–8; *add. solum* ܡܚܝܢܐ 2, 13, 21 **51** ܕܡܫܡܫܝܢ] *add.* ܒܫܡܟ *omnes minus* 1, 2 ܠܡܕܒܚܟ] *add.* ܩܕܝܫܐ 41; *add.* ܗܢܐ ܩܕܝܫܐ *ceteri minus* 2, 4, 7, 9, 15 (*incertum* 3) **52** ܘܡܨܠܝܢ] *om. waw* 1, 22 **53** ܫܒܚܝܢ] *add.* ܘܪܘܡܝܢ 3–4, 7 ܘܡܪܡܪܡܝܢ] *om.* 10, 14, 17–18 ܘܡܣܓܕܝܢ] ܘܣܓܕܝܢ 2, 4

40 which we offer to thee upon the pure and holy altar, as thou hast taught us,

41 and make with us thy tranquillity and thy peace all the days of the age,

42 (*Response* Amen)

F

43 *Priest* that all the inhabitants of the world may know thee,

44 that thou alone art God the true Father,

45 and thou didst send our Lord Jesus Christ thy Son and thy Beloved,

46 and he, our Lord and our God, taught us in his life-giving Gospel

47 all the purity and holiness of the prophets and apostles and martyrs and confessors

48 and bishops and priests and deacons,

49 and of all the children of the holy catholic Church,

50 those who have been signed with the sign of holy Baptism.

G

51 And we also, O my Lord, thy unworthy, frail, and miserable servants, who are gathered and stand before thee,

52 and have received by tradition the example which is from thee,

53 rejoicing and glorifying and exalting and commemorating

ܘܡܒܪܟܝܢ ܠܗ ܠܐܪܙܐ ܗܢܐ ܪܒܐ ܘܕܚܝܠܐ. 54
ܕܚܫܗ ܘܕܡܘܬܗ ܘܕܩܝܡܬܗ ܕܡܪܢ ܝܫܘܥ ܡܫܝܚܐ. 55

H

ܘܢܐܬܐ ܡܪܝ، ܘܪܚܡܢ ܩܕܝܫܐ. ܘܢܬܬܢܝܚ ܟܠ ܩܘܪܒܢܐ 56
ܗܢܐ ܕܒ̈ܢܝܢ.
ܘܢܒܪܟܘܗܝ، ܘܢܫܒܚܘܗܝ،. ܕܢܗܘܐ ܠܝ ܡܪܝ، ܠܚܘܣܝܐ ܕܚܘܒ̈ܐ. 57

ܘܠܫܘܒܩܢܐ ܕܣܟ̈ܠܘܬܐ. ܘܠܚܘܒܪܐ ܪܒܐ ܕܡܫܟܢܬܐ ܕܥܡ ܒܢܝ̈ 58
ܫ̈ܡܝܬܐ.
ܘܠܫܝܢܐ ܫܪܝܬܐ ܒܡܠܟܘܬܐ ܕܫܡܝܐ ܥܡ ܟܠ ܕܫܦܪܘ ܩܕܡܝܢ. 59

I

ܘܥܠ ܒ̈ܢܝ ܟܠܗ ܡܕܒܪܢܘܬܟ ܬܫܒܘܚܬܐ ܕܠܥܠܡ. 60
ܢܘܕܐ ܠܟ ܘܢܫܒܚܟ ܕܠܐ ܫܠܘܐ. 61
ܒܕܬܟ ܦܪܘܩܬ ܒܕܡܗ ܢܦܫܐ ܕܡܫܝܚܟ. 62

ܒܦܘܡܐ ܦܬܝܚܐ ܘܒܦ̈ܘܡܐ ܫ̈ܠܝܬܐ. 63
ܟܕ ܡܩܪܒܝܢ ܬܫܒܘܚܬܐ ܘܐܝܩܪܐ ܘܬܘܕܝܬܐ ܘܣܓܕܬܐ. 64
ܠܐܒܘܟ ܚܝܐ ܘܩܕܝܫܐ ܘܡܚܝܢܐ. 65
ܗܫܐ ܘܒܟܠܙܒܢ ܘܠܥܠܡ ܥ̈ܠܡܝܢ. 66
ܐܡܝܢ. R 67

54 ܘܕܚܝܠܐ] *om.* 2, 81: *add.* ܘܩܕܝܫܐ ܘܐܠܗܝܐ 2, 4–5, 8–10, 12, 14–18, 20–4, 28[a], 33, 41, 78, 81, 85–6; *add. praeterea* ܘܡܫܝܚܝܐ *post* ܘܩܕܝܫܐ 10, 14, 17–18, 20–3, 41, 78, 81, 85–6 **55** ܘܕܡܘܬܗ] *add.* ܘܕܩܒܘܪܬܗ 2–5, 7–10, 12, 14, 16–17, 19, 22–4, 28[a], 33, 41, 78, 85–6. ܕܡܪܢ] *add.* ܦܪܘܩܢ 5, 9, 10, 11 (*ut vid.*) 12, 14, 16–17, 19, 22–3, 78, 85–6 **56** ܘܢܐܬܐ] *om. waw* 1, 24, 33, 78: ܘܬܐܬܐ 6, 17 ܩܕܝܫܐ] *pr.* ܘ ܚܝܐ 4, 6, 11 (*ut vid.*) 12, 24, 28[a], 33, 86 **59** ܥܡ . . . ܩܕܡܝܢ] *om.* 4, 9 **60** ܡܕܒܪܢܘܬܟ] ܡܕܒܪܢܘܬܐ 6, 8, 10–11, 13–14, 17, 19, 20, 22–3, 78, 85; *add. praeterea* ܗܕܐ ܪܒܬܐ ܘ 8, 10, 13–14, 19–20, 22, 78, 85 **61** ܢܘܕܐ] *pr. dalath* 4, 6, 41 **63** ܘܒܦ̈ܘܡܐ] *om. beth* 4, 24, 78

54   and celebrating this great and awesome mystery

55   of the passion and death and resurrection of our Lord Jesus Christ.

H

56   And let thy Holy Spirit come, O my Lord, and rest upon this offering of thy servants,

57   and bless it and sanctify it that it may be to us, O my Lord, for the pardon of sins

58   and for the forgiveness of shortcomings, and for the great hope of the resurrection from the dead,

59   and for new life in the kingdom of heaven with all who have been pleasing before thee.

I

60   And for all thy wonderful dispensation which is towards us

61   we give thee thanks and glorify thee without ceasing

62   in thy Church redeemed by the precious blood of thy Christ,

63   with open mouths and unveiled faces

64   offering glory and honour and thanksgiving and adoration

65   to thy living and holy and life-giving name,

66   now and at all times and for ever and ever.

67 *Response* Amen.

Textual Notes

A

No variants of any importance have been recorded in this section. In many MSS there are substantial abbreviations where only *incipits* are provided; this is most common in ll. 3–4 and 6. Only in MSS 77 and 86, where the last two words alone of l. 6 ('the glorious King') are omitted, is there any probability that this represents a genuine variant. Otherwise all MSS that have a full text are in agreement with what is printed here.

B

10 At the end of the line the majority of MSS add ܘܣܓܕ̈ܬܐ ܘܪܘܡܪܡܐ ܡܢ ܟܠ ܒܪ̈ܝܢ ('and adoration and exaltation from all creatures'), the only ones without any addition being six Ḥudra MSS (1–3, 7–8, 15) and MS 4. There are, however, some variations. Four MSS (5–6, 21, 36) omit ܘܪܘܡܪܡܐ ('and exaltation'); five others (17, 54, 72, 77, 79) add ܘܡܝܩܪܐ ('and excellency') after ܪܘܡܪܡܐ; MS 6 substitutes ܦܘ̈ܡܐ ('mouths') for ܒܪ̈ܝܢ ('creatures') in assimilation to the earlier phrase; and MS 9 substitutes the cumbersome ܕܒܪܐ ܘܡܬܥܒܕ ܒܫܡܝܐ ܘܒܐܪܥܐ ('which is created and made in heaven and earth'). In view of this variety in the additional matter and its complete absence from so many of the oldest MSS, it is all regarded as secondary expansion of the original text.

11 After ܡܫܒܚܬܐ many MSS add ܕܬܠܝܬܝܘܬܐ ܡܫܒܚܬܐ ('of the glorious Trinity'), while a smaller number add a second-masculine- singular suffix to ܬܠܝܬܝܘܬܐ, turning the phrase into a direct address to God ('of thy glorious Trinity'). Since none of the Ḥudra MSS has either form of this addition, and of those in Group B only MSS 16 and 81 have one each, it too is regarded as a secondary expansion of the original text. The omission of *dalath* ('of') in ܕܐܒܐ ('of the Father') is a consequential adjustment to the suffixed form of this addition, and is found exclusively in MSS with this reading. The prefixing of *dalath* to both ܒܪܐ ('the Son') and ܪܘܚܐ ('the Spirit') is made in a dozen or so MSS, mostly of the Alqosh and Chaldaean traditions. The addition of *dalath* to ܪܘܚܐ only in MSS 1, 16, 41, 78, and 84 is illogical. Since only one Ḥudra MS (15) and none of those in Group B has *dalath* with both words, the addition is regarded as secondary.

12 A few MSS, including two Ḥudra ones (8, 41), read *seyāmē* with ܥܠܡܐ, treating the word as plural ('the worlds'). The originality of this

reading is belied by its inconsistency with the singular suffix to ܘܥܡܘ̈ܪܝܗ,
('and its inhabitants').

13 The omission of the clause ܘܦܪܩ . . . ܒܚܘܣܢ ('and redeemed the sons
of men in his mercy') in three of the Malabar MSS (25, 68, 71) is secondary
and probably the result of scribal error. The transposition of the last two
words of this clause is found only in MS 16 and is contrary to the word order
in the two previous clauses. Neither of these variants is at all probable.

C

14$^{1°}$ The fuller text ('bless and adore') has the support of three Ḥudra MSS
(8, 11, 41), all those in Group B, and all the unclassified ones except MS 21.
The shorter text is found in most Chaldaean MSS, but most tellingly in the
oldest Ḥudra MSS (1–3, 7, 15), and for this reason the fuller text has been
adjudged the result of a typical secondary expansion.

14$^{2°}$ The addition of ܩܕ̈ܝܫܐ ('holy') to ܡܠܐܟ̈ܐ ('angels') is practically
universal, but a few of the older MSS read instead ܡܩܕܫܝܢ ('hallowing'),
while MS 41 is unique in reading both. The variation between the two
additions in the oldest MSS suggests that both are alternative secondary
expansions, and in this case the reading without addition, although attested
solely by MS 1, has been judged original.

15$^{1°}$ The prefixing of *waw* to ܡܫܡ̈ܫܢܐ ('the ministers') has some early
attestation, including three Ḥudra MSS, and has the effect of making this
phrase a further category of supernatural beings rather than a general
description of the foregoing categories. The attestation seems hardly sufficient, however, to warrant the adoption of this reading, which could have
arisen accidentally in assimilation to the two previous *waws*.

15$^{2°}$ The last two words of this line ('glorifying thy name') are omitted at
this point in MSS 1, 9, and 12, but read before ܕܩ̈ܥܝܢ ('crying out') in **16**
in MSS 1, 9, and 11, MS 9 adding further the word ܘܡܝܩܪܝܢ ('and
honouring'). At the same point in **16** MSS 12 and 54 read ܠܥܕܝ̈ܟ ܡܩܕܫܝܢ
ܘܡܫܒ̈ܚܝܢ ('hallowing and praising thy name'), while a few MSS (17, 27, 33,
86) substitute ܡܩܕܫܝܢ ('hallowing') for ܡܫܒ̈ܚܝܢ ('glorifying') in **15**.
The substitution of ܡܩܕܫܝܢ for ܡܫܒ̈ܚܝܢ in either position is probably
an assimilation to the approaching *Sanctus* (cf. already the minority
addition in **14**$^{2°}$). Similarly MS 41 adds ܩܕ̈ܝܫ ('holy') after ܫܡܟ
('thy name') in **15**. The presence of ܠܥܕ̈ܝܟ ܡܫܒ̈ܚܝܢ here in the majority
of the oldest MSS is accepted as evidence that this is probably the original
reading.

16$^{1°}$ Although the *waw* before ܥܡ ('with') has some early and wide later
attestation, its absence from most of the Ḥudra and older Group B MSS
marks it as secondary.

16$^{2°}$ The transposition of ܘܣܪ̈ܦܐ ('and the seraphim'), and ܩܕ̈ܝܫܐ

('holy') and the addition of ܪܘܚܐ ('spiritual'), yielding the text ܟܪܘܒܐ ܩܕܝܫܐ ܘܣܪ̈ܦܐ ܪܘܚܢܐ ('the holy cherubim and spiritual seraphim') is widely attested, but its absence from all the Ḥudra MSS except MS 11 stamps it as a secondary modification. The secondary nature of the further addition ܡܩܪܒܝܢ ܣܓܕܬܐ ܠܪܒܘܬܟ ('offering adoration to thy majesty') is marked also by the substitution of variations on ܐܪܥܐ ܘܫܡܝܐ (see above on 15²°) and by the prefixing of yet further material ܕܠܐ ܫܠܝ ܒܐܡܝܢܘ ('without ceasing continuously') in MSS 4 and 28 and partly also in MS 23.

18 In most MSS the *Sanctus* is indicated only by an *incipit*. The printed text of this line is that of MS 3, the oldest to contain a full text. A full text is found also in MSS 4–5, 23, 27, 47, 50, 56, 62, 74, 81, 85, and 86. The main variations are the insertion of ܐܠܗܐ ('God') between ܡܪܝܐ ('Lord') and ܚܝܠܬܢܐ ('Almighty') in MSS 4–5, 81, 85, and 86 (an insertion found nowhere in the biblical MSS of the Peshiṭta of Isa. 6: 3), and the omission of ܡܢ ('of') in MSS 5, 27, 50, 56, 62, 74, and 86, probably in assimilation to the Peshiṭta text. The omission of the third ܩܕܝܫ ('holy') in MSS 4 and 47 is probably accidental, and the reading of ܡܠܐ ('full') in the singular rather than the plural in MS 47 is probably an error.

In some MSS a *Cushapha* follows, which begins with the text of **18**, sometimes with the insertion of ܐܠܗܐ (e.g. in MSS 6, 12, 16, 23–24, and 33) and sometimes without (e.g. in MSS 10 and 17), and MS 59 omits ܡܢ. MS 56, however, has neither ܐܠܗܐ nor ܡܢ in the *Sanctus*, but both in the following *Cushapha*, which indicates that it is hazardous to draw inferences from the *Cushapha* as to the text of the *Sanctus* implied in cases where only an *incipit* of the latter is given. MS 23 too has no ܐܠܗܐ in the *Sanctus*, but has it in the *Cushapha*.

Macomber (1966, p. 363, n. 9) draws attention to the fact that although the Mar Esh'aya Ḥudra text of the Anaphora of Addai and Mari contains only an *incipit* for the *Sanctus*, the text of the Anaphora of Theodore in that MS contains a full text of the *Sanctus*, of which Macomber's note gives a Latin rendering, including the word *Deus* between *Dominus* and *omnipotens*. In the photocopy of the transcript of the Mar Esh'aya text of the Anaphora of Theodore which Dr Macomber kindly sent me, however, the word ܐܠܗܐ does not occur, the text of the *Sanctus* agreeing exactly with that of **18** of the text printed in this edition.

19–20 Even fewer MSS contain the *Hosanna*. The text printed is that of MSS 5, 56, 81, and 85 (which adds *waw* before the second ܐܘܫܥܢܐ in **19**). MS 47 contains a slightly corrupted form of the same text.

Macomber's note mentioned above is correct in indicating that the *Hosanna* follows the *Sanctus* if it is a festival. The text of the *Hosanna* in the Anaphora of Theodore according to the Mar Esh'aya Ḥudra is slightly different from that of **19–20** of the text printed in this edition of the

Anaphora of Addai and Mari. Macomber's Latin is an accurate rendering of the Syriac text:

ܐܘܫܥܢܐ ܒܡܪ̈ܘܡܐ . ܒܪܝܟ ܕܐܬܐ ܘܐܬܐ
ܒܫܡܗ ܕܡܪܝܐ . ܐܘܫܥܢܐ ܠܒܪ ܗ ܕܕܘܝܕ.

'Hosanna in the highest! Blessed is he who has come and comes in the name of the Lord. Hosanna to the Son of David!'

D

23 The omission of the second word in MSS 2 and 4* is almost certainly an error, caused perhaps by partial assimilation to **13**.

26 The omission of the first two words in MS 16 and the Chaldaean MSS is surely a mechanical error, and is chiefly of interest as suggesting a link between MS 16 and the Chaldaean tradition.

30 After this line twelve MSS (2, 4–6, 11, 12–13, 17, 21, 23, 28, 56) insert various parts of the following: ܚܢܢܐ ܘܡܚܣܝܢܐ ܕܚܘܒܐ ܘܒܘܨܪ̈ܐ ܚܣܐ ܠܝ ܚܘܒܝ ܘܒܘܨܪ̈ܝ, ܒܛܝܒܘܬܟ / ܒܝܘܡܐ ܕܕܝܢܟ ('O merciful One and forgiving of sins and shortcomings, forgive me my sins and shortcomings by thy grace in the day of the/thy judgement'). Despite the early attestation of parts of this, it is regarded as secondary for the following reasons:

(a) its total omission in many MSS, including some early ones (1, 3, 7–10, 15–16, 19, 22, 24, 33, 41, 81);

(b) the considerable variety of selections from it in the MSS that do contain part of it;

(c) the fact that it breaks the natural sequence from **30** to **31**;

(d) the fact that in spirit, if not in form, it resembles the *Cushapha* prayers (note the first-singular suffixes in ܠܝ, ܚܘܒܝ, ܘܒܘܨܪ̈ܝ).

33 A few Chaldaean MSS (43–4, 56) insert an additional canon at the end of this line; it is marked as optional in MSS 44 and 56.

E

38 Ten Chaldaean MSS (55, 59–61, 63, 67, 70, 82–4) prefix what is evidently a secondary insertion: ܠܒܬܘܠܬܐ ܡܪܝܡ ܝܠܕܬ ܐܠܗܐ ܘ ('the Virgin Mary, bearer of God, and').

39 MSS 3 and 7 read the second and third words in the emphatic state, but this is a purely stylistic difference, and the reading with suffixes is more idiomatic.

40 The reading ܡܕܒܚܐ without suffix ('the altar') is found in seven of the Ḥudra MSS, three of those in Group B, and four of the unclassified MSS.

The reading ܡܕܒܚܟ with suffix ('thy altar') is a natural development with some early attestation, but the weight of the earliest evidence is decisively in favour of the form without suffix. The reading with a third-masculine-singular suffix ('his altar') in MSS 24 and 33 is an interesting variant, and possibly a deliberate modification, the antecedent being Christ at the end of the previous line. The singular reading ܕܐܠܦܢ ('as he taught us') in MS 4 may be similarly inspired.

41 The reading ܘܥܒܕܬ ('and thou hast made') in MSS 3 and 8 is probably an assimilation to the previous word; the context requires an imperative rather than a perfect indicative.

42 The *Amen*, which occurs only in MSS 1, 6, 11, 21, and 81 (preceded by ܐܦ ܘ ('yea and') in MSS 6, 21, and 81), does not mark the end of a prayer, since the sense of **41** is continued in **43**. Some MSS go straight from **41** to **43** (3, 7–8, 12–13, 15, 41, etc.), some with a note to repeat **41**; many repeat it after prefixing ܐܦ ܡܪܢ ܘܐܠܗܢ ('yea, our Lord and our God') (4–5, 10, 16–17, 24, etc.), and this form alone is found instead of **41** in MSS 2 and 9. These variations are best explained as diverse attempts to emphasize **41**, the *Amen* without elaboration or any repetition of **41** being regarded as the simplest and earliest form.

F

44 The omission of ܐܒܐ ('the Father') in MSS 8 and 24 is hardly likely to reflect the original text; if it is not a mere error, it could be explained as a deliberate assimilation to the text of John 17: 3, to which the line alludes.

46[1°] The addition of a ܐܬܐ ܘ ('came and') before ܐܠܦ ('taught') is widely attested, but its absence from the Hudra MSS, three of those in Group B, and three of the unclassified MSS seems decisively to favour the shorter text.

46[2°] The omission of the last two words in MS 16 and the Chaldaean MSS is hardly likely to reflect an original text, but, like the reading in **26**, suggests a link between MS 16 and the Chaldaean tradition.

A further minor variant in **46** is the reading ܘܗܘܝܘ at the beginning of the line picked up by *dalath* before the verb ('and it is he . . . who'); this is found in MSS 2 and 21, and MS 2 further omits the intervening words ('our Lord and God').

47 The omission of the third word in MS 13 is probably an error. Nor is the substitution of *lamadh* for *dalath* in the series from the fourth word of **47** to the first word of **49** in MS 21 likely to be original.

48 The omission of the first word in MS 6 may have been occasioned by the insertion of the additional category of leaders ('and teachers'), the varying position of which (before or after the bishops) betrays its secondary nature.

50[1°]   The addition of ‎ܚ̈ܝܐ‎ ('living') is almost universal, but the fact that a number of significant MSS add ‎ܘܡܚ̈ܝܢܐ‎ ('and life-giving'), while others read ‎ܡܚ̈ܝܢܐ‎ alone, arouses the suspicion that both adjectives are secondary expansions, and that the original reading of MS 1 was correct in reading neither. See also the next note.

50[2°]   The omission of the last word in MSS 13, 61, and 79 is probably secondary. MS 15, however, reads the adjective in the masculine with the first noun ('with the holy sign of Baptism'), a transposition possibly inspired by an exemplar in which ‎ܪܘܫܡܐ‎ had no adjective (as in MS 1*).

G

51[1°]   The addition of ‎ܒܫܡܟ‎ ('in thy name') after ‎ܕܡܬܟܢܫܝܢ‎ ('who are gathered') in all MSS except 1 and 2 must give a high probability to the originality of the reading, which is of some importance in the history of the exegesis and literary criticism of the anaphora. On the other hand, the omission of the word in the two oldest witnesses, together with the intelligibility of the text without it, must raise serious doubts about its originality, and it cannot bear the weight of any hypothesis such as that of Botte (1949, 1965).

51[2°]   The addition of ‎ܒܙܒܢܐ ܗܢܐ‎ ('at this time') at the end of this line is slightly less well attested. Its omission in three of the Ḥudra MSS and the two oldest in Group B, together with the attestation of the noun only in MSS 31 and 41, raise grave doubts about its originality.

52   The omission of *waw* at the beginning of the first word in MSS 1, 22, 31, and 39 is likely to be secondary, and may have arisen as a deliberate modification in order to provide a main verb in Section G. The form with only one *nun* in MSS 10, 25, and 51 is an orthographic variant.

53[1°]   The *waw* at the beginning of the line in MSS 6, 11, and 61 is a secondary assimilation to the series of *waw*s in the context.

53[2°]   The addition of ‎ܘܪܘܙܝܢ‎ ('and exulting') in three early MSS, like that of ‎ܘܡܫܒܚܝܢ‎ ('and praising') at different points in MSS 1 and 23, is no doubt a secondary amplification.

53[3°]   The omission of ‎ܘܡܪܝܡܝܢ‎ ('and exalting') in four early MSS and in those of the Malabar tradition is also likely to be secondary.

53[4°]   The Pe'al stem of the verb ('and remembering') found in two of the oldest MSS may be felt to cohere more closely with the noun ‎ܥܘܗܕܢܐ‎ ('commemoration') from this stem found in **39**. On the other hand the Aph'el stem ('commemorating') is a natural form to use of the solemn *anamnēsis* of the Eucharist. The transposition of this word and the previous one in three of the latest Chaldaean MSS (82–4) is probably a simple copying error.

54 The addition of further adjectives ('and holy (and life-giving) and divine') to the two at the end of the line is a further example of secondary expansion. In addition to the combinations cited in the apparatus are the following: ܘܐܠܗܝܐ ܘܩܕܝܫܐ in MS 2 (omitting ܘܕܚܝܠܐ itself), ܘܩܕܝܫܐ ܘܡܫܒܚܐ (ܡܫܒܚܐ meaning 'glorious') in MS 6, and ܘܩܕܝܫܐ ܘܡܫܒܚܐ ܘܐܠܗܝܐ ܘܡܚܝܢܐ in MSS 21 and 81 (again omitting ܘܕܚܝܠܐ). The two adjectives printed in the text are found without further addition in MSS 1, 3, 7, and 11 (*ut vid.*), and this is thought to be the most likely original text from which the other readings have been expanded.

551° The addition ('and burial') is widely attested, but its absence from four Ḥudra MSS (1, 11, 13, and 15) and also from MSS 6 and 81 raise serious doubts about its originality.

552° The addition ('and our Redeemer') is also widely attested, but its absence from eight Ḥudra MSS, four in Group B, and three of the unclassified MSS raises even more serious doubts about its originality.

H

561° The evidence for the omission of the *waw* at the beginning of the line is slight, but significant, in MSS 1, 24, and 33. The feminine form of the verb, found only in MSS 6 and 17, reflects the older use of feminine verbs with ܪܘܚܐ, even when it denotes the Holy Spirit, but its originality in this context is belied by the three following masculine verbs; the two at the beginning of **57** are feminine only in the idiosyncratic MS 54.

562° The addition ('living and') is found in one Ḥudra MS (11 *ut vid.*), four in Group B, and three of the unclassified ones, but the evidence is quite inadequate to establish its originality. It seems to be a typical expansion.

563° The reading ܕܩܘܕܫܐ (literally 'of holiness') for the adjective ܩܕܝܫܐ ('holy') in MS 9 is an interesting survival of an older usage found also in **2**.

564° The addition of ܘܢܫܪܐ ('and dwell') before (MS 9) or after (MS 16) ܘܬܬܢܝܚ ('and rest') is shown, by its varying position, to be secondary.

565° A diaconal interjection ܗܘܝܬܘܢ (ܘܒܕܚܠܬܐ) ܒܫܠܝܐ ('Be in stillness (and awe)') is inserted at different points in a number of MSS, but is absent completely from many others (see Macomber's apparatus for details). Its absence from many of the oldest MSS, the different positions at which it is inserted, and the fact that it breaks the natural sequence of the prayer suggest that it is a secondary 'aside', and it has therefore not been included in the text or apparatus of this edition.

57 The *waw* in place of *dalath* at the beginning of the third word in MSS 23 and 54 is a simple corruption.

591° The omission of the last four words in MSS 4 and 9 is an interesting coincidence, but hardly likely to attest an original shorter text. The omission of ܠܟ ('all') in MS 81 is an error, since it leaves the following *dalath* without an antecedent.

59[2°] The substitution of a third- for the second-masculine-singular suffix in the last word ('him' for 'thee') in MSS 16 and 21 and most of the Chaldaean MSS is improbable, since one would have to go back at least to **56** for an antecedent to the third-person suffix.

I

60[1°] The reading ܡܒܪܘܬܟ with suffix is found in six of the Ḥudra MSS, seven of those in Group B, and three of the unclassified MSS, as well as in most of those of the Chaldaean tradition. It seems thus to be the better attested of the two readings among the oldest MSS, although the reading without suffix, often with the addition of ܗܢܐ ܪܒܬܐ ܘ ('this great and'), is found in some early MSS as well as in those of the Alqosh and Malabar traditions.

60[2°] The reading ܫܒܝܚܬܐ ('glorious') in place of ܬܗܡܘܪܬܐ ('wonderful') in MSS 17 and 31, the omission of ܕܠܘܬ ('which is towards us') in MSS 7 and 79, and the addition of ܕܠܐ ܡܬܦܪܥܐ ('which cannot be repaid'), as in **23** in MS 81, are all inferior.

61 The reading of *dalath* before the first word, though attested in three significant MSS and three of the Chaldaean MSS, is unsatisfactory because by making this a dependent clause it deprives Section I of a main clause.

63 The omission of *beth* in the third word in MSS 4, 24, 35, and 78 is probably simply an error.

COMMENTARY

THE main purpose of this Commentary is literary-critical and historical. Although textual criticism enables us to recover only a medieval text of the Anaphora of Addai and Mari, it is possible at several points to make comparisons with other anaphoras and with documentation in catechetical and other non-liturgical sources. The questions with which we are concerned throughout the Commentary are what, if any, evidence can be found to indicate that the medieval text has undergone modification from an earlier form, and how far the earliest form attainable is compatible with an origin as early as the third century.

In the case of those parts that are widely paralleled in other anaphoras (the opening dialogue, the *Sanctus* with its introduction, and the *epiklēsis*), specific comparisons make a tentative dating possible. The case of the *epiklēsis* is particularly instructive, for there we find the closest parallel in Hippolytus, and the oldest core of the *epiklēsis* has the appearance of being distinctly earlier than that of Serapion. In the case of the opening dialogue there is much to suggest that it was originally closer in form to that of Hippolytus, while the *Sanctus* appears in a form closer to that of the biblical text than that of Serapion. Where the most direct comparisons are possible, therefore, the Anaphora of Addai and Mari appears to date from a period between Hippolytus and Serapion, and its affinities with Hippolytus are closer than those with Serapion.

Engberding (1932) drew attention to several similarities between Sections B–D of the Anaphora of Addai and Mari and the Anaphora of Chrysostom. We have noted parallels to the inclusion of redemption as well as creation in the pre-*Sanctus* (ll. 12–13), although there is no significant verbal agreement, and to the restriction of the heavenly beings mentioned in ll. 14–16 to the thousands and myriads of Dan. 7: 10, the cherubim, and the seraphim of Isa. 6: 2, where the verbal agreement is the result of the use of common biblical sources. Two points of similarity where there is significant verbal agrement are the beginning of the post-*Sanctus*

(l. 21 'And with these . . . hosts') and the beginning of the first doxology (l. 31 'And for all'). These common elements are not enough to prove any direct relationship between the anaphoras, but they probably do reflect a distant relationship within the wider Syrian 'family', without providing any indications of the date of the Anaphora of Addai and Mari.

Insufficient attention has been paid to the sixth-century fragment edited by Connolly (1925). Despite the many lacunae and obscurities in this text, for some of which Connolly provides convincing restorations, a number of parallels have been noted to significant phrases in the Anaphora of Addai and Mari: the 'name' of God (l. 11), 'we also' (l. 22), 'benefits' (l. 31), 'upright and just' (l. 38), 'peace' (l. 41), and 'mystery' (l. 54). At one point (Sections E–F) we have ventured to use the fragment as a partial basis for attempting a reconstruction of an obscure passage in the Anaphora of Addai and Mari (see the Appendix, with discussions in the Commentary on Sections E–F and G). It is not possible at present to trace the relationship between the fragment and the three extant East Syrian anaphoras, so that once again no indications of the date of that of Addai and Mari are afforded by the parallels in the fragment.

By far the most important liturgical text with which the Anaphora of Addai and Mari must be compared is the Maronite Anaphora of Peter III, generally known as *Sharar*. There are fairly close parallels between the two anaphoras in Sections B–D and H–I and also in two short passages within Sections E–F. Engberding (1932, p. 46) claimed as the result of an examination of the two anaphoras extending over Sections B–D that *Sharar* throughout offered the older and more original version of the common text underlying them both. Botte (1965, p. 98), however, dismissed as an illusion the belief that *Sharar* takes us back to an older and purer form of the intercessions, arguing that since *Sharar* is an adaptation, its evidence, when it diverges from the Anaphora of Addai and Mari, proves nothing about the original structure of the anaphora. Macomber (1971, p. 84) reaffirmed the importance of *Sharar* for the study of the Anaphora of Addai and Mari, and claimed that the elements common to the two anaphoras must be very ancient indeed. Macomber (1982) attempted a reconstruction of the common source of the two anaphoras. He admitted (p. 75) that he made a basic assumption which cannot be proved: that the common elements were already present in the common form before each Church began to develop the anaphora independently. This seems to be a reasonable working hypothesis. It may be felt in general, however, that he has given too much relative weight to *Sharar*, and has underestimated the implications of the extent to which it has later been overlaid (p. 78) for the task of reconstructing the supposed common source.

In this Commentary the view has been taken that where fairly close parallels exist, it is generally possible within narrow limits to reconstruct the original common core, but that where the two anaphoras diverge substantially, it is much less practicable to do so. An examination of the detailed differences between the two anaphoras in the most closely parallel passages has not led to the conclusion that either has in general preserved the original text more faithfully. On the contrary, now the one and now the other has proved to contain the more probably older text. Moreover, some of the elements in *Sharar* that have no parallel in the Anaphora of Addai and Mari seem to reflect a later theological position (e.g. the adjective 'propitiatory' attached to the word 'altar'). Where the two anaphoras differ within the closely parallel passages, each text has to be evaluated separately. The relationship between the two anaphoras is a matter for literary, rather than textual, criticism. There is every reason to believe, however, that the common core, where it can be reconstructed with reasonable probability, is at any rate earlier than the separation of the Churches after the Council of Ephesus in 431. An attempted reconstruction of the earliest attainable form of the whole of the anaphora, drawing occasionally on other sources in addition to this common core, may be found in the Appendix.

Is it possible to reach any more precise indications of the date of the Anaphora of Addai and Mari? One factor arising out of the comparison with *Sharar* which may have a bearing on this question is the further question to whom the anaphora is addressed: to the Father, the Son, or the Blessed Trinity? The chief evidence for the last possibility is the reading in l. 11 which has been adjudged secondary on textual grounds. At this stage the celebrant still refers to God in the third person, and the Trinitarian reference in the authentic text of l. 11 is not unnatural. Direct address to God begins only at l. 14, and no conclusions of a Trinitarian address may be drawn from the *Sanctus*. The chief evidence for the prayer being addressed to the Son is in l. 24, which clearly refers to the Incarnation. There are also the references to the institution of the Eucharist in ll. 40 and 52. On the other hand, there are unequivocal references to Christ in the third person in ll. 39, 45–6, 55, and 62, and the reference to the Holy Spirit in l. 56 is also in the third person. The overwhelming impression therefore is that the anaphora is addressed to the Father, unless we are to assume several changes of Person addressed within the prayer, without any clear indication that this is the case. An explanation, particularly of l. 24, is sometimes sought in a modalist theology, which, if well grounded, would point to an early-third-century date. It is possible that l. 24 does belong to the oldest stratum of the anaphora and does reflect a modalist theology. One might also argue, however, that the initiative for the whole economy of redemption is ascribed to the Father, on the lines of 2 Cor. 5: 19, and that the direct language of l. 24, and *a fortiori* of ll. 40 and 52, is to be explained in this light. The fact that *Sharar* is throughout, even in the Institution Narrative, addressed to the Son is sometimes seen as evidence that the common core of the two anaphoras was also addressed to the Son. If that were the case, it is hard to see why the reformulation of the Anaphora of Addaï and Mari in terms of address to the Father was carried out in such a way as to leave the ambiguities of ll. 24, 40, and 52. It seems much more likely that it is *Sharar* that has consistently modified the common core so as to maintain a constant address to the Son. We have seen already (in Section B of the Introduction) that Origen regarded the address of the anaphora to the Father as an unbroken tradition. Yet the fact that the Council of Carthage of 297 (Canon 23) required the anaphora to be addressed to the Father indicates that this was not universal practice towards the end of the third century. It seems best to regard the Anaphora of Addaï and Mari as addressed to the Father, and to explain ll. 24, 40, and 52 either in terms of a modalist theology or perhaps more probably simply in terms of a lack of sophistication in Trinitarian theology which would be natural in the first part of the third century, but increasingly less so with the progress of time. It is certainly impossible to maintain that the anaphora is addressed to the Son in its present form on the hypothesis of a partial reformulation of an originally consistent address to the Son.

Further indications of a relatively early date may be sought in other general characteristics of the anaphora. The Semitic parallelism, particularly noticeable in the original core of Sections B, D, and H, has often been remarked. The Semitic idiom ܪܚܡܥܠ ܝܣ ('deal graciously') in ll. 13 and 23 should also be noted. Little weight, however, can be attached to such factors in assessing the date of the anaphora. Any Christian liturgical text composed directly in Syriac would be likely to display such characteristics, which are a reflection partly of the nature of the language and partly of the biblical background. The anaphora is further characterized by an economy of expression, an avoidance of verbose elaboration, and a concentration on essentials (see Engberding, 1932, p. 40), which are readily compatible with an early date, but hardly adequate to establish it. The accumulation of praise words in ll. 32, 53, and 64, which might be thought to suggest a later date, are paralleled in the Mishnaic passage from *Pesahim* 10. 5 quoted in the Commentary on Section D below, and are thus no obstacle to an early date.

The anaphora contains a substantial number of biblical allusions. Direct use is made of 2 Cor. 13: 14 in ll. 1–2, of Isa. 6: 2 in ll. 16–18, and of Matt. 21: 9 in ll. 19–20. These, however, are all passages widely attested in liturgies outside the East Syrian family, and cannot be used as specific evidence for the use of biblical material in this anaphora. In addition to a number of less specific allusions noted in the Commentary, we may draw attention here to the most striking allusions in the anaphora: Dan. 7: 10 (l. 14), Ps. 104: 4 (l. 15), 1 Sam. 2: 7 (l. 25), Eph. 1: 18 (l. 27), John 17: 3 (ll. 43–5), Deut. 10: 8 (l. 51), Isa. 11: 2 (l. 56), Eph. 3: 21, Acts 20: 28, and 1 Pet. 1: 18–19 (l. 62), and 2 Cor. 3: 18 (l. 63). In the case of the allusion to John 17: 3 in ll. 43–5 it may be wondered whether there is also a reminiscence of 1 Kgs. 8: 60 as suggested by Vellian (1972, p. 215), although there is little verbal agreement with the Peshitta of that verse. To illustrate how subtle a biblical allusion can be we may recall the last word of 37, ܡܩܒܠܐ ('gracious', literally 'acceptable'), which has been deemed a secondary element in the text because it is absent from the parallel passage in *Sharar*. Whatever its origin, it is probably ultimately inspired by a reminiscence of Mal. 1: 10, a favourite passage among the early Christians, who saw in it a prophecy of the 'acceptable' nature in God's eyes of the Christian Eucharist in contrast to the Jewish sacrifices which were no longer 'acceptable' to him (cf. Justin, *Dialogue with Trypho*, 41: 2–3; 117).

The fact that Basil found it necessary to urge the use of biblical language in the praise of God (as we have seen in Section B of the Introduction) suggests that he was aware of a lack of due use of scriptural material in anaphoras he encountered on his travels. This might in turn imply that the relatively high use of scriptural material in the Anaphora of Addai and Mari is an indication of a relatively later date. On the other hand, the deficiency of which Basil was aware may not have obtained in a different region, and in any case the use of Scripture in this anaphora is allusive rather than precise, and has the appearance of being semi-conscious rather than deliberate or contrived. Altogether it seems doubtful whether the biblical material in the content of the anaphora throws any more light on its date than its general economy of expression or its Semitic colouring.

Another question that may have an important bearing on the date of the anaphora is that of its structure. It is noteworthy that the anaphora is divided into two by the first doxology in ll. 31–3. Vellian broke new ground in his suggestion that the anaphora corresponds in structure to the two benedictions preceding the recitation of the *Shema'* in the Jewish morning service, rather than to the three Jewish meal blessings as suggested by Bouyer (cf. our discussion in Section A of the Introduction). His main reasons for preferring a correlation with the benedictions preceding the *Shema'* are the absence of any reference to food and the division into two rather than three units, each ending with a doxology. Sections A–D of the anaphora are thus regarded as the counterpart of the benediction *Yoṣer*, and Sections E–I of the benediction *Ahabah*.

It is true that thanks are offered for creation in Section B and that the *Sanctus* is used in Section C, but the nearest equivalent Vellian can find to the theme of creation of light is the enlightening of the understanding in l. 27, which we have seen to be an allusion to Eph. 1: 18. On the other hand, redemption, which is a dominant theme in Section D of the anaphora, finds only faint echoes in *Yoṣer*: 'Shield of our salvation . . . our King and Redeemer . . . causes salvation to spring forth'. The parallel to l. 10 which Vellian finds in the prayer preceding *Yoṣer* in the Sabbath morning service is to be explained in terms of common dependence on Isa. 45: 23. In short, there is no verbal correspondence that cannot be explained in the light of common dependence on biblical material, while the distribution of thanksgiving for creation and redemption in the two texts is in inverse proportion.

The most striking point in common between Sections E–I and the benediction *Ahabah* is the mention of the ancestors. In the Jewish benediction, however, the prayer is that God will be gracious to the present community for the sake of the fathers, while in the anaphora the prayer is that God will remember for good the fathers themselves in the context of the eucharistic commemoration of the body and blood of Christ (ll. 36–40). The prayer for peace in the anaphora (l. 41) is linked with that for the universal knowledge of God (l. 43), but in the Jewish benediction it is linked rather with the gathering of the dispersion. The main theme of the Jewish benediction is the gift of Torah, to which the nearest parallel Vellian can find in the anaphora is the reference to the command to celebrate the Eucharist (l. 40).

In the light of this analysis it is surprising to read Vellian's conclusion (p. 216):

Excepting the epiklesis, we find a common structure to the Addai and Mari and to the *yotzer* and *ahubah berakoth*, taken together. Invitation to praise, commemoration of the creation, praising with the angelic hymn, and doxology form the first part. The second part remembers gratefully the love of God in giving his commandments (Torah in *ahubah rabbah*, or to repeat what he has done in Addai and Mari), and the rest of the economy of salvation—the fathers, the land and the forming of a people. Both of them end with a doxology.

As we have seen, the parallels are in fact of the most general kind, and it has not been demonstrated that either in its overall structure or in detailed correspondences the anaphora shows any real evidence of having been modelled on the benedictions. In the course of a sympathetic discussion of Vellian's hypothesis, Spinks (1977, pp. 148–52) points out that even some of the parallels to the anaphora that Vellian finds in *Yoṣer* and *Ahabah* (the *Sanctus* and the prayer for peace) are not extant in the Genizah fragments and may therefore be secondary elements within the Jewish benedictions. This weakens Vellian's argument still further.

The presence of a doxology in the middle of the anaphora may not after all be so problematic. A partial parallel to ll. 31–3 may be found in the Anaphora of Chrysostom (*LEW*, p. 322, ll. 13 ff.), although this occurs at a relatively earlier point, before the *Sanctus*. A closer parallel may be found (with Engberding, 1932, p. 45) at a later point in the Anaphora of Chrysostom (*LEW*, p. 329, ll. 7, 9), at the point of transition from the *anamnēsis*-oblation to the *epiklēsis*. In both passages in the Anaphora of Chrysostom the doxological material forms a climax to a series of thanksgivings, since the Institution Narrative which leads into the *anamnēsis*-oblation is itself part of the thanksgiving for redemption. Similarly the doxology in ll. 31–3 in the

Anaphora of Addai and Mari is the climax of the thanksgiving for creation and redemption which has dominated Sections B–D.

If we were to stress the concluding character of these doxological passages, we might be inclined to speculate that they reflect a period when the whole of the Eucharistic Prayer consisted of thanksgiving (incorporating elements of *anamnēsis* and perhaps an Institution Narrative), before the addition of such elements as intercession and *epiklēsis*. In that case Sections A–D would represent the oldest strata of the anaphora, which would have been subsequently extended by the addition (probably in several stages) of Sections E–H, Section I being a resumption and expansion of the doxology of ll. 31–3 to conclude the whole. It must be stressed, however, that such a reconstruction of the evolution of the prayer must remain speculative since, had it occurred, it would have antedated the oldest document-ation available to us. On the other hand we have to note that the failure to demonstrate a close correspondence with the Jewish benedictions *Yoṣer* and *Ahabah* removes a further potential argument for a very early, even a second-century, date for the anaphora.

One further question requires consideration before we can proceed to the detailed commentary on the text of the anaphora section by section. This concerns the absence from the textual tradition of the anaphora of any Institution Narrative, probably the feature of the anaphora that has excited the greatest attention from liturgists. There is evidence, according to Macomber (1982, p. 83, n. 13), for the insertion of an Institution Narrative at at least four different points in the rite. Two of these are within Section D of the anaphora itself. The 1901 missal of the Chaldaean Catholics inserted it apparently after l. 22, while the Anglican Urmia edition of 1890, followed by the restored Malabar missal of 1960, inserted it after l. 30. There is no inherent likelihood for an Institution Narrative in either of these positions. Bishop Roz, followed by the Malabar and Chaldaean Catholic missals, inserted it just before the Elevation preceding the Fraction (*LEW*, p. 290, col. 2, l. 1), while the supplementary fo. 101a in MS 16 seems to intend it to be inserted before the Blessing following the Fraction and other manual acts (*LEW*, p. 293, l. 15). All of these are secondary insertions, and it remains true that there is no extant MS authority for the inclusion of an Institution Narrative in the text of the anaphora. The alternative possibilities are therefore that the anaphora originally contained an Institution Narrative which was subsequently lost, or that it never contained one in the first place.

Those who argue for the first possibility have to answer the question how an original Institution Narrative came to be lost. It must first be noted that *Sharar* contains an Institution Narrative within that part of the anaphora in which the two texts diverge sharply (corresponding to ll. 41–6 of the Anaphora of Addai and Mari). It is questionable whether *Sharar* can be regarded as providing evidence for the hypothetical lost common core at this point. In the commentary on Sections E–F below we show reasons for doubting the originality of *Sharar* at this point. On the other hand, the comparison of the two anaphoras demonstrates the existence of a common-core text of the greater part of the anaphora before the separation of the Churches in the fifth century. This has the effect of confining the possible parts of the anaphora in which an Institution Narrative might once have existed to the passages in which the two anaphoras diverge (ll. 41–6 and 51–5).

Macomber (1982, pp. 81 f.) regards the first of these two positions as the likely one. This is the point at which the text of the intercessions in the attested form is confused, where he thinks that a Chaldaean reviser of the supposed original common core of the two anaphoras united the first and second references to the fathers, and in so doing passed over the intervening Institution Narrative and *anamnēsis*, which in his opinion survived only in *Sharar*. He suggests that the Chaldaean reviser may have regarded the Institution Narrative as no longer important in comparison with the *epiklēsis*. He considers further the possibility, already proposed in Macomber (1971, pp. 56, 74, and 1977a, pp. 112 f.), that the Chaldaean reviser in question was the patriarch Isho'yabh III of the mid-seventh century. According to Ibn aṭ-Ṭayyib (d. 1043; for text see CSCO 167–8, pp. 90 and 93), this patriarch abbreviated the anaphora, and this seems to offer objective evidence for the reduction of an originally longer text in the course of which an Institution Narrative may have been lost. On the other hand, Engberding (1932, p. 47) points out the difficulty of reconciling this tradition of abbreviation in the seventh century with the demonstration of the existence of a common-core text which can be traced back to a time before the separation of the Churches in the fifth century. Accordingly he questions the accuracy of the tradition recorded by Ibn aṭ-Ṭayyib, and suggests that it may rest on no more than a knowledge that Isho'yabh had been a liturgical reformer. Our own study of ll. 41–6 suggests that they are more primitive than the longer material at the corresponding point in

Sharar, which contains several features suggesting that it originated at a period later than that of the common core. It is possible then that the present confusion in ll. 41–6 is the result of abbreviation, but it is unlikely that *Sharar* preserves an earlier form of the text before abbreviation, and there is no positive reason for assuming that an Institution Narrative once formed part of the intercessions at this point. How likely the omission of an existing Institution Narrative might be in the seventh century is in itself a matter for debate.

Botte's hypothesis that l. 51 presupposes a now lost Institution Narrative which it once immediately followed is examined in detail in the Commentary on Section G. The verbal link he thought to trace with the Institution Narrative is weakened by the absence of the word ܒܫܡܟ ('in thy name') from l. 51 in the two oldest MSS, and his theory also suffers from his failure to establish a main verb so that Section G can stand satisfactorily on its own. Three alternative explanations of the 'we also' in l. 51 are possible in addition to Botte's suggestion that it contrasts the present congregation with the original disciples at the Last Supper. In any case the general considerations offered above against the probability of the loss of an original Institution Narrative in the course of abbreviation apply with equal force here.

The Anaphoras of Theodore and Nestorius both contain an Institution Narrative with *anamnēsis* attached to the post-*Sanctus* and before the intercessions. These anaphoras, however, as we have seen (Introduction, Section C), were translated from the Greek and offer no direct evidence for an original Institution Narrative in the Anaphora of Addai and Mari. Indeed the common core of this anaphora and *Sharar* proceeds directly from the post-*Sanctus* to the intercession (see the Commentary on Sections E–F), indicating that in the early fifth century at any rate there was no Institution Narrative at this point. The real significance of the presence of the Institution Narrative in the texts of the Anaphoras of Theodore and Nestorius is that it demonstrates that there was no aversion to a written text of the Narrative, and thus undermines the suggestion that the absence of an Institution Narrative from the actual MSS of the Anaphora of Addai and Mari is explicable on the grounds that it was recited secretly (cf. Raes, 1944, p. 225).

Raes (ibid., p. 224) also draws attention to the somewhat unusual Institution Narrative in the sixth-century fragment edited by Connolly (1925, p. 112, ll. 20–35), of which a translation is given here:

And because he was about to be taken up from our place and exalted to the place of the spiritual beings from which he had come down, he left in our hands a pledge of his holy body, that through his body he might be near to us and at all times be united to us through his power. For before the time of his crucifixion and the hour in which he was about to be glorified he took bread and wine which his will had made, (and) made it holy with a spiritual blessing. And he left this awesome mystery to us, and allowed us a good likeness, that we should continually do as he did, and live through his mysteries.

Despite the fact that a lacuna follows immediately, the passage may possibly be complete as it stands. It does not contain the dominical words, but it does narrate that the Lord took bread and wine and sanctified them, and it does contain a reference to our doing as he did. Raes thinks that it is not an Institution Narrative, but only a mention of the Institution, but this seems to do less than justice to it. Its significance for our purpose is that it seems to stand half-way between a full Institution Narrative of the normal kind, in which the dominical words are quoted, and the kind of allusion to the Last Supper that is to be found in ll. 39–40 and 52 of the Anaphora of Addai and Mari. As such it may serve to strengthen the possibility that these clear, but concise, allusions to the Last Supper were felt to be sufficient to establish the connection between it and the eucharistic celebration. Raes (1970, pp. 6–7) points out that the celebration of the saving acts of God in Christ in the post-*Sanctus* concentrates on the benefits of redemption as a whole rather than on the historical stages of Incarnation, Passion, and Resurrection, through which it was wrought, for which we may compare the succinct summary in l. 55. In the light of this the absence of a formal Institution Narrative seems more intelligible.

At this point it is worth recalling that some recent studies have questioned the assumption that an Institution Narrative was practically universal. Cutrone (1978) offers as an explanation of the fact that Cyril of Jerusalem in *Cat. Myst.* 5. 6–7 goes straight from the *Sanctus* to the *epiklēsis* the possibility that his anaphora did not contain an Institution Narrative at all. Other explanations are possible, as he recognizes, and perhaps more probable, but at the very least this evidence discourages dogmatism that an Institution Narrative was regarded as an indispensable element in an anaphora in the mid-fourth century. If it is true that the Institution Narrative only gradually came to be regarded as essential, its absence from the

Anaphora of Addai and Mari may be an indication of the relatively early date of that anaphora.

None of these lines of exploration has led to any certainty that the earliest attainable form of the Anaphora of Addai and Mari, viz. the common core of that anaphora and *Sharar*, dates from the second or early third century. On the other hand, we have found no evidence to preclude such an early date, and if we are right in detecting even a tendency towards modalism in the manner of the address of the anaphora, this would point to such a date. The several points of similarity to the *Apostolic Tradition* of Hippolytus also point in that direction. The lack of sufficient early material for comparison and the lack of other specific indications preclude a more definite dating. The possibility remains, however, that the Anaphora of Addai and Mari is the earliest actual anaphora extant, and it is almost certainly the earliest still in regular use.

A

The first eight lines of the text constitute the opening dialogue between celebrant and congregation. The oldest text of this dialogue is that recorded in Hippolytus' *Apostolic Tradition*:

P.	Dominus vobiscum.	The Lord be with you.
R.	Et cum spiritu tuo.	And with thy spirit.
P.	Sursum corda.	Lift up your hearts.
R.	Habemus ad Dominum.	We lift them to the Lord.
P.	Gratias agamus Domino.	Let us give thanks to the Lord.
R.	Dignum et iustum est.	It is meet and right.

It is immediately apparent that this dialogue consists of a greeting or blessing followed by two exhortations, to each of which the people make a response. A general survey of variations in the dialogue has been given by Bouman (1950), while a detailed analysis of variations in the opening greeting has been made by Engberding (1929).

The East Syrian liturgies adopt the Pauline greeting of 2 Cor. 13: 14, which Engberding finds to be characteristic of Byzantine liturgies. There are two distinctive modifications in the East Syrian liturgies. The first is the replacement of 'you' by 'us', turning the greeting into a prayer for blessing of priest and people, with the corollary that the people's response is changed from a mutual greeting to a simple

'Amen'. The second is the addition of the phrase referring to the time for which the blessing is asked, found in l. 3 of our text.

Comparison between ll. 1–2 and the Peshitta text of 2 Cor. 13: 14 reveals some interesting facts. The Peshitta's replacement of 'grace' by 'peace' finds no place in the anaphora. On the other hand, the addition of 'the Father' in the anaphora is not to be found in the Peshitta. Only in the suffix to *Maran* ('our Lord') do the anaphora and the Peshitta agree against the Greek New Testament. However, when the text of the anaphora is compared with the Byzantine text (*LEW*, p. 321, ll. 14–16) they are found to be in almost exact agreement. Apart from the modification of 'you' to 'us', the only difference is the absence from Addai and Mari of the 'and' between 'God' and 'Father' in the Byzantine text. It seems reasonable to conclude that both the addition of 'Father' and the supply of the verb 'be' reflect derivation from the Greek-speaking liturgical tradition rather than an independent adoption of the greeting from the biblical text.

The text cited in Theodore of Mopsuestia's *Mystagogical Lecture* 16 (pp. 98 f. and 236 f. in Mingana's edition) is in close agreement with the Byzantine text. The wording of the greeting is practically identical with ll. 1–2 of Addai and Mari except for the reading 'you', while the response is the traditional ܘܥܡ ܪܘܚܟ ('And with thy spirit') as in the Byzantine text.

Hippolytus' Latin text of the second exchange finds corroboration in the allusion of Cyprian (*De Oratione* 31). Cyril of Jerusalem quotes this formula in what may well have been the original Greek of Hippolytus: ἄνω τὰς καρδίας . . . ἔχομεν πρὸς τὸν κύριον (*Cat. Myst.* 5. 4), for the Latin is an exact translation of this text. Two modifications are found in the Greek liturgical tradition. The addition of a verb σχῶμεν ('Let us have') in the Byzantine rite (*LEW*, p. 321, l. 20) is rightly recognized by Bouman as secondary and formed on the analogy of the response. The supply of the verb 'be' in Addai and Mari seems to be an independent amplification. The other is the replacement of τὰς καρδίας by τὸν νοῦν already in *Apostolic Constitutions* 8 (*LEW*, p. 14, l. 17), a modification no doubt intended to bring out the sense of the Semitism 'hearts'. This modification would hardly seem necessary in a Syriac text, and the use in Addai and Mari of a word meaning 'your minds', albeit retaining the primitive plural, suggests again the influence of Greek usage. The text of this exchange quoted by Theodore of Mopsuestia is particularly interesting (Mingana, pp. 99 and 238). To the exhortation of the priest: ܢ ܩܕܡ ܠܠ the people respond: ܡܪܝܐ ܠܟ ('To thee, O Lord'). The exhortation is identical with that of Addai and Mari except that it lacks the latter's insertion of the verb 'Let . . . be', and is interesting in that it shares the plural noun 'minds' against the Greek use of the singular when 'mind' is substituted for 'hearts'. The response is even more noteworthy since it departs radically from the traditional form, but has every appearance of being a more primitive form from which the actual response in Addai and Mari has been expanded. We have no criteria to establish the ultimate priority of Hippolytus' or Theodore's response, although the earlier and much wider attestation of the former must stand in its favour.

The final exhortation seems to derive ultimately from Jewish meal graces (*Berakoth* 7. 3, Danby, p. 8), and thus to constitute the oldest element in the opening dialogue. The response generally formed the cue for the exordium of the Eucharistic Prayer itself, as e.g. in the Byzantine text (*LEW*, p. 321, l. 28 (Chrysostom) and p. 322, l. 1 (Basil)), *Apostolic Constitutions* 8 (*LEW*, p. 14, l. 25), and by implication also the *Euchologion* of Serapion, which does not contain the dialogue itself. Theodore similarly records the exchange: ܘܗܘ ܡܪܐ ... ܐܪܐ ܘܗܘܡ (Mingana, pp. 99 and 238). The retention of the traditional response in l. 8 of Addai and Mari creates the presumption that the present l. 7 is a replacement for the original formula as in Theodore's quotation. Narsai's *Homily* 17 (Connolly, 1909, p. 12) alludes to the present text of l. 7, but we do not know when or why it was substituted for the traditional formula.

Macomber (1971) draws attention to the dialogue prefatory to the blessing of the baptismal oil, where the final exhortation takes the form: ܢܘܕܐ ܘܢܣܓܘܕ ܘܢܫܒܚ ܠܐܠܗܐ ܡܪܐ ܟܠ ('Let us give thanks and adore and praise God the Lord of all') (Kelaita, p. 136). He points out that the three verbs in this exhortation correspond to the two nouns and two adjectives in the exordium of the Eucharistic Prayer of Addai and Mari (ll. 10–11), and rightly concludes that this was the earlier formula before it was displaced by the announcement 'The offering is being offered'. It seems to be an expansion of the primitive exhortation. Macomber's further suggestion that this statement was originally the opening of the dialogue, put forward tentatively on the basis of very limited parallels in *Sharar* and reaffirmed in Macomber (1982) with only a minor modification, is far less convincing, especially in view of the weight of evidence for an almost universal greeting at the beginning of the dialogue. It is surely *Sharar* that is eccentric here.

Too much weight should probably not be given to the at first sight startling replacement for the traditional formula in l. 7. It is worth remembering that *Qurbana* is the normal East Syrian term for the Eucharist, and that its meaning is hardly different from that of the Greek word ἀναφορά. The congregation are simply being informed, in the customary terminology, that the moment has arrived for the Eucharistic Prayer to begin. The basic meaning of the root *qrb* is to 'draw near', and in the intensive theme it means to 'offer' or 'present', with such varied objects as 'remarks' and 'advice' as well as more cultic terms. It is familiar in an essentially non-cultic sense from the Corban of Mark 7: 11. What is offered varies widely according to the context in which the verb is used, from the money implied in the Gospel narrative to the praise and thanksgiving which the sequel in ll. 10–11 suggests are the essential content of the Eucharistic Prayer of Addai and Mari. It is thus not unreasonable to claim that no essential difference of meaning is intended from that of the traditional exhortation. See also the more complex argument adduced by Spinks (1980, pp. 24 f.).

It is not easy to know how to evaluate the evidence of the quotations in Theodore's *Mystagogical Lecture* 16. Lietzmann has demonstrated that the liturgy presupposed by Theodore belongs to the Antiochene Syrian type and has particularly close relations with that of *Apostolic Constitutions* 8. The main interest in the first and third exchanges is that we have here a Syriac version of the traditional forms with which we can compare the text of Addai and Mari. It is only in the second response that Theodore departs radically from the Antiochene or Byzantine forms, and it is precisely here that his agreement with the fundamental form of the response in Addai and Mari is so interesting. It can hardly be explained as the Syriac translator's modifications of Theodore's text to conform with that familiar in the East Syrian anaphoras, since it is inconceivable that such a modification if attempted at all should be carried out to such a limited extent. Our conclusion above that Theodore's second response is the earlier form which has been expanded in Addai and Mari seems sound.

It seems reasonable then to conclude that the present text of the opening dialogue of Addai and Mari represents a modification of an earlier form in several important respects. This earlier form was probably derived ultimately from the liturgy of a Greek-speaking community, whose affiliations were with what became the Antiochene and/or Byzantine family, although the text may well have been rendered into Syriac during the oral stage of transmission. An opening dialogue is only feasible if the people's responses are fixed and the priest's part is clearly recognizable (cf. the expanded forms of the two exhortations in the Anaphoras of Theodore and Nestorius). The variations between different formularies mostly reflect variations of usage in different geographical areas (so Engberding, 1929). Within this overall pattern the East Syrian variations are more extensive than most. Apart from the tendency to expansion seen most clearly in Addai and Mari in ll. 3 and 6, the chief modifications are the alteration of the opening exchange from a mutual greeting into a prayer for the blessing of all with a congregational *Amen*, and the substitution of the *Qurbana* formula for the ancient one reflecting the language of the Jewish meal blessings. This last instance, together with the evidence throughout the rest of the dialogue of ultimate derivation from Greek forms, indicates that in the opening dialogue the Anaphora of Addai and Mari has drifted somewhat away from its Semitic moorings.

The diaconal intervention of l. 9 seems also to be a secondary element, since it breaks the sequence between the presumed original text of l. 7 and the exordium of the Eucharistic Prayer itself in ll. 10–11. It is however clearly an 'aside', and the inclusive 'with us' is in harmony with the 'us all' of l. 2.

NOTES ON THE TRANSLATION

2 'Holy Spirit': literally 'Spirit of holiness', as in the Old Testament idiom. The same idiom occurs in 11, but in 56 the adjective 'holy' is used, probably because a suffix ('thy') is attached to 'Spirit' in that passage.

4 'for ever and ever': literally 'to the age of the ages', for which cf. the very similar phrase 'to the ages of the ages' in Greek and Latin liturgical texts.

5 'hearts': literally 'minds' (see above, pp. 77–8).

B

This is the first section in which a detailed comparison with *Sharar* is possible. Engberding (1932) devoted considerable attention to this passage, but the availability of critical texts of both anaphoras reduces both the similarities and the differences that emerged from the texts available to him. As it stands, the paragraph falls into two major divisions: ll. 10–11 state the appropriateness of praise to God in a way that immediately suggests that it is a sequel to the introductory dialogue, while ll. 12–13 give the fundamental grounds for this in brief statements of the creative and redemptive acts of God. As it stands, furthermore, the whole section is a statement about God in the third person: note especially the three third-person verbs and the three third-masculine-singular suffixes ('his') in ll. 12 and 13. Only at Section C (if authentic) or D does the direct address to God begin. The passage seems therefore to be a continuation of the opening dialogue, in which God is for the most part spoken of in the third person, and this is one of the most distinctive features of the Anaphora of Addai and Mari.

The only element in l. 10 that finds a parallel in *Sharar* is the noun ܫܘܒܚܐ ('praise'), but even this occurs in quite different connections. On the other hand, l. 11 is virtually identical in the two anaphoras, the only difference being the use of *dalath* before the Son and the Spirit as well as the Father in *Sharar* (found also in some MSS of Addai and Mari; cf. the textual note on l. 11). In *Sharar* ܫܘܒܚܐ in the nominative is the opening word, and it is followed by *lamadh* with a second-masculine-singular suffix ('to thee') and then immediately by l. 11, which thus becomes a direct address to God. Besides the awkward address to the name of God rather than simply to God, the secondary nature of this text is betrayed by the retention in *Sharar* of the third person throughout ll. 12–13. Engberding points out that this acclamation form is unusual at the beginning of the Eucharistic Prayer, but nevertheless regards it as relatively closer to the original form than the exordium of Addai and Mari.

In Addai and Mari ܫܘܒܚܐ is itself introduced by *lamadh* after the opening ܫܘܐ ('Worthy'). This word itself is problematic, since it is not one of the actual words used in the response in l. 8, whereas it is the word corresponding to *Dignum* in the West Syrian anaphoras. In fact neither of the terms used in l. 8 would be suitable for use in direct relation to God or even the name of God, while ܫܘܐ is the natural word for such a context. The Greek and Latin words can be used in either sense, although in fact *Vere Dignum* is generally the predicate of infinitives expressing the praise of God. The statement that God or the name of God is worthy of praise is thus another distinctive feature

of Addai and Mari. The *Dignum–Vere Dignum* connection is thus not
verbally present in Addai and Mari, though it seems reasonable to
suggest that a similar logical sequence links the exordium to the
opening dialogue. Ledogar (1968, p. 28) points out that the *Vere
Dignum* connection is probably a secondary development in the
anaphora. It is found in Serapion, but not in Hippolytus, where the
connection with the opening dialogue is with the third exhortation
rather than with the people's response: 'Gratias agamus Domino . . .
Gratias tibi referimus' ('Let us give thanks to the Lord . . . We give
thee thanks'). The connection in Addai and Mari may thus be a very
early form.

It is interesting to speculate whether the use of ܐܘܐ in the final
response of the West Syrian opening dialogue is a secondary
replacement for the East Syrian ܐܪܐ to facilitate the connection with
the exordium of the prayer, or whether ܐܘܐ in l. 10 of Addai and
Mari points as Engberding suggests to an original ܐܘܐ in l. 8.
Engberding regards ܐܘܐ as a sign of the West Syrian origin of the
present beginning of l. 10. He also dismisses as secondary expansion
the remainder of l. 10 after the first two words (which in his text
includes the additional material mentioned at the beginning of the
textual note on l. 10) which, as we have seen, has no counterpart in
Sharar. Once however the secondary nature of the direct address to
the name of God in *Sharar* is recognized, a more favourable view may
be taken of l. 10 of Addai and Mari. Its originality may be defended
on the grounds of (a) its Semitic parallelism, (b) its allusion to Isa. 45:
23, and (c) the centrality of ܬܘܕܝܬܐ ('thanksgiving') to the prayer as
a whole. The second and third of these points will be taken up below.

Both anaphoras ascribe the praise in l. 11 not directly to God, but
to the name of God. Engberding notes that this is a Semitic feature,
and compares the sixth-century fragment edited by Connolly (1925,
p. 102, l. 27 and p. 104, l. 7). He thinks it may well ultimately reflect
Jewish influence. Macomber (1982) thinks that the last four words of
l. 11 are a secondary anti-Arian insertion. Ratcliff (1929) draws
attention to the reminiscence of Phil. 2: 9–11 in ll. 10–11, and points
out that the name in that passage is that of Christ. This he links with
his theory that the anaphora was originally addressed to Christ. This
argument, however, though followed by Macomber, is far from
conclusive. Behind the text of Phil. 2: 9–11 lies Isa. 45: 23, where the
homage of every knee and every tongue is to God himself. There is
moreover ample Jewish background to the concept of hallowing the

name of God, as is patent from studies of the Lord's Prayer in relation especially to the *Kaddish* Prayer. One may also draw attention to Mal. 1: 11, which was frequently applied to the Eucharist by early Christian writers (e.g. Justin, *Dialogue with Trypho* 41. 2–3). Only if it could be proved beyond doubt that *Sharar*'s address to the Son belonged to the common core of the two anaphoras would it be reasonable to take the name here as that of Christ. Spinks (1980) rightly points out that there is nothing in l. 11, shorn of the later accretion mentioned in the textual note, that could not be derived from Matt. 28: 19, and one may note further that this line is a natural counterpart to the Trinitarian greeting of ll. 1–2, also couched in scriptural language.

Before leaving ll. 10–11, it remains to comment briefly on the terminology of praise. These two lines contain words from three roots denoting aspects of praise. ܣܓܕ means literally to 'bow oneself' or 'do reverence', and thus more generally to 'adore' or 'worship'. Ledogar (p. 18) points out that it corresponds to the Greek προσκυνεῖν. ܫܒܚ, on the other hand, has a wider range of meaning and is used to translate δοξάζειν, αἰνεῖν, ὑμνεῖν, and even on occasion εὐχαριστεῖν (ibid.). The basic meaning of the verb is to 'praise' or 'glorify', but it has not proved practicable to use a single English equivalent consistently in the translation. As far as possible 'glory' and 'glorify' have been used to render words from this root, but 'praise' has been used for the noun ܫܘܒܚܐ in l. 10 and 'glorious' for the participle ܡܫܒܚܐ in l. 11.

The noun ܬܘܕܝܬܐ is from the root ܝܕܐ, the Aph'el of which is used in the basic sense of 'confess' or 'acknowledge' while the precise sense varies according to the context and may refer to a profession of faith, an acknowledgement of sin, or an offering of thanksgiving. The same range of meaning is found in the cognate Hebrew הודה. It is the word used in Theodore of Mopsuestia's citation of the final exhortation of the priest in the opening dialogue, where the rendering 'Let us give thanks' is appropriate (cf. the Greek and Latin counterparts), and the fact that reasons for thanksgiving follow in ll. 12–13 make the same meaning the most appropriate here. The same contextual argument points to a rendering in the sense of thanksgiving in ll. 21, 32, 61, and 64, where the root recurs. See also Ledogar, pp. 21, 157 f., where it is pointed out that the Aph'el of ܝܕܐ and its cognate noun are used regularly to render the ὁμολογεῖν group, and also εὐχαριστεῖν in the New Testament.

The text of *Sharar* available to Engberding was much closer at this point to that of Addai and Mari than that in Sauget's critical text, although Engberding's fuller text is to be found as the reading of *ceteri* in his apparatus. The only substantial difference was the absence in *Sharar* of the adjective ܪܒܐ (lit. 'great') in l. 13. The same idiomatic expression recurs in l. 23, where again the adjective is absent from *Sharar*, but present in Addai and Mari (on the few exceptions in each passage see above, p. 41). It is reasonable to suppose that in both passages the adjective is a secondary expansion which has occurred only within the East Syrian tradition. For the rest, Engberding notes the absence of any descriptive praise of the being of God, the inclusion of redemption as well as creation in the pre-*Sanctus* (for which he compares especially Chrysostom: *LEW*, p. 322, ll. 6–13), and the absence of elevated language. The concentration on bare essentials he deems a mark of high antiquity, a judgement with which we concur.

The text of *Sharar* published by Sauget differs considerably from that of Addai and Mari after the first four words of l. 12. The next three words have no counterpart, and then ܠܛܝܒܘܬܐ is replaced by ܩܢܘܡܗ and ܒܛܝܒܘܬܗ (as in l. 12) is repeated at the end of l. 13. This must be rejected as an inferior text. Not only does Addai and Mari preserve the symmetry of parallelism in both lines, while the second is compressed in *Sharar* to a single clause, but *Sharar* has broken up the elements of the semitic idiom ܥܒܕ ܛܝܒܘܬܐ = עשׂה חסד = 'deal graciously', to which the preposition ܥܠ ('with'), corresponding to the Hebrew עם, is appropriate, substituting the awkward ܥܒܕ ܦܘܪܩܢܐ ('effected redemption'). This has all the appearance of an unsuccessful attempt at restoration of the text after a mechanical omission.

What is stressed in ll. 12–13 is that the creative and redemptive acts of God are evidence of his grace. Three words are used, one of them twice. ܡܪܚܡܢܘܬܐ, like its Hebrew cognate, is related to the word for 'womb', and expresses the concept of parental love. ܛܝܒܘܬܐ basically means 'goodness' and hence 'kindness', but as we have seen it is used with the verb ܥܒܕ as the idiomatic equivalent of the Hebrew עשׂה חסד meaning 'deal graciously', and we have also seen that it is used in l. 1 to render the Greek χάρις. ܚܢܢ, like its Hebrew cognate, also suggests the idea of grace and favour, but perhaps with stronger overtones of mercy and pity. It is unlikely that any very clear demarcations of meaning are intended between these different terms in the present passage.

Section B of Addai and Mari emerges then from a comparison with the parallel passage in *Sharar* as much closer to the common original text, only the adjective ܪܒܐ in l. 13 being probably a secondary accretion. The parallelism, the Semitic idioms, and the concentration on bare essentials all suggest that this is a very early text indeed.

NOTES ON THE TRANSLATION

10 lit. 'from all mouths . . . from all tongues'.
13 lit. 'effected great grace towards'; the idiom has necessitated the paraphrase: 'dealt very graciously with'.

C

The origins of the liturgical use of the *Sanctus* in both Judaism and Christianity are obscure. The one indubitable fact is that the text of the *Sanctus* itself derives from Isa. 6: 3. Baumstark (1923) drew attention to three minor modifications of the biblical text in its Christian liturgical usage:

(*a*) a change from the third person to the second in the final word: 'his glory' becomes 'thy glory';

(*b*) the insertion of the word 'God' between 'Lord' and 'of hosts';

(*c*) the change of 'the whole earth' into 'heaven and earth'.

Of these the first is a necessary change when the formula is used in direct address to God, and the second is found in Old Latin texts of Isaiah. Flusser (1963) draws attention to the probable Jewish background of the third in the Qumran text 1QH 16. 3, and suggests that it rests on an exegesis of the word 'whole' in the biblical text. Cf. also the Targum of Isa. 6: 3.

Van Unnik (1951) demonstrated the improbability of any direct reference to Eucharistic worship in the celebrated allusion to Isa. 6: 3 in 1 Clement 34. 6 f., and the *Sanctus* is absent from the 'model' Eucharistic Prayer of Hippolytus. It occurs in Serapion with the first and third, but not the second, of the modifications noted by Baumstark. It occurs in *Apostolic Constitutions* 8 (*LEW*, p. 18, l. 32–p. 19, l. 1) with only the third of these modifications.

The additions of *Hosanna* and *Benedictus qui venit* are not found in the Egyptian liturgies. Baumstark suggested that the *Benedictus* was a deliberate substitution for Ezek. 3: 12, which was attached to Isa. 6: 3

in the Jewish benediction *Yoṣer*, which precedes the recitation of the *Shemaʿ* in the daily morning prayer. He drew attention to the common element εὐλογημένη/εὐλογημένος in the two additions to Isa. 6: 3, suggesting that Christian usage substituted a Christological benediction from the New Testament for the passage from Ezekiel, which lent itself to interpretation in terms of the Jerusalem Temple. He suggested that an earlier substitute for Ezek. 3: 12 may have been Rom. 1: 25, as in *Apostolic Constitutions* 8 (*LEW*, p. 19, l. 2). Baumstark drew attention further to two secondary developments in the Christian text of the *Benedictus* and *Hosanna* in the Syriac-speaking area. The first is the double interpretation of ὁ ἐρχόμενος as 'who has come and comes', while the second is the expansion of the *Hosanna* with the phrase 'Hosanna to the Son of David' (cf. Matt. 21: 9 and perhaps *Didache* 10. 6) in the East Syrian rite.

The hymn of praise in Isa. 6: 3 is attributed to the seraphim, but in the Eucharistic Prayer this is generally expanded to include other angelic beings, often with verbal use of Dan. 7: 10. Spinks (1980a) has drawn attention to a number of Jewish texts, particularly the 'Angelic Liturgy of Qumran', which indicate that the angelic speculations of the Jewish Merkabah mystical tradition are pre-Christian in origin. However difficult it may be to establish a direct link between Jewish and Christian angelology and liturgical use of the *Sanctus*, it seems increasingly probable on general grounds that the earliest Christians were already familiar with the liturgical use of the *Sanctus* in Judaism, and that the modification 'heaven and earth' in particular is of Jewish origin.

Turning to the text of the *Sanctus* in l. 18 of the Anaphora of Addai and Mari, we note that this differs form the Peshiṭta of Isa. 6: 3 essentially only in the third of the modifications listed by Baumstark, the only one for which we have found Jewish evidence. The other differences from the Peshiṭta text are the consequential plural of the adjective 'full' and the stylistic insertion of the preposition ܡܢ ('from') before the final word. Three features taken over from the Syriac text of Isaiah may also be mentioned. ܚܝܠܬܢ is a common equivalent of צבאות ('of hosts'), corresponding to the Septuagint παντοκράτωρ. This is here a noun rather than an adjective, and we have rendered it by the title 'Almighty'. It is interesting that the text cited by Theodore (Mingana, pp. 100 and 239) differs from that of l. 18 only in the omission of ܡܢ and the transliteration ܣܒܐܘܬ (*Sabaoth*) in place of ܚܝܠܬܢ. The insertion of the relative particle *dalath* before the second clause and the rendering in the plural of the last word (literally 'whose glories') are the other two features taken over from the Syriac text of Isaiah. There is some, but hardly sufficient, evidence in the MSS (see the textual note on l. 18) for the second of Baumstark's modifications, while the total absence of any evidence for his first one suggests that the *Sanctus* here is even more primitive than that found in Serapion. In common with the Jewish use of the *Sanctus* in *Yoṣer*, the third of the *Eighteen Benedictions*, and the *Kedusha de Sidra*, the *Sanctus* here is not yet turned into a direct address to God.

Lines 19–20 correspond fairly closely to the Old Syriac and Peshiṭta of Matt. 21: 9, the last two words being anticipated also at the beginning of l. 19. The enclitic ܐܘ after ܒܪܝܟ ('Blessed') is suppressed, and the only other difference is the double interpretation of ܐܬܐ already noted (for which cf. the Syriac Liturgy of St James; *LEW* p. 86, l. 16). This double rendering probably refers to the Incarnation and the Eucharist. In our translation we have retained the traditional 'in the highest' for ܒܪܘܡܐ, which means literally 'in the heights' or 'on high'.

We turn now to the question of the originality of the *Sanctus* in the Anaphora of Addai and Mari. Ratcliff (1929) regarded the *Sanctus* as an interpolation on the grounds that the clauses introducing it have no connection with what precedes them, and that 'the whole passage coming in between an address of praise to the Creator and Redeemer and a thanksgiving for salvation and grace is out of place.' The first four words of l. 21 are also deleted as a secondary link after the insertion of the *Sanctus* with its introduction. This argument is accepted by Botte (1949) with the additional point that redemption is mentioned already in l. 13, but picked up only in ll. 24 ff., and reaffirmed in Botte (1965), with the further point that the first four words of l. 21 and the first word of l. 22 are absent from *Sharar*. The excision of the whole of Section C, together with the five words from ll. 21–2, yields in his opinion a perfectly coherent text.

These arguments are by no means convincing. Macomber (1982) defends the originality of the *Sanctus* on the grounds that it does not interrupt the sequence of thought. Interpreting the inhabitants of the world in l. 12 as comprising both angels and humans, he suggests that the worship of the angels is first expressed in Section C, reaching its climax in the *Sanctus*, and that this is followed by the thanksgiving of humanity, ll. 21–2 relating the two together. To this argument may be added the point that the transition from the third to the second person is much more abrupt if l. 21 follows immediately on l. 13, whereas in Section C the transition is made more gradually in that while God is now addressed directly the focus is on the description of the worship of the angels in the third person, leading into the descriptive third-person form of the *Sanctus*. The transition to the direct worship of the earthly congregation then follows neatly in ll. 21–2. These arguments may be felt to be a sufficient refutation of Ratcliff's objections to the originality of the *Sanctus* and to the first of Botte's additional points.

Macomber (1982) further draws attention to the fact that although the five connecting words in ll. 21–2 are absent from *Sharar*, it does contain the *Sanctus* itself, and also the phrase 'we thy sinful servants' in the immediate sequel; the emphatic repetition of the pronoun 'we' in both texts indicates that the contrast between the worship of heaven and that of the earthly congregation belongs to the common core of the two anaphoras. A reason is suggested below for the absence of the connecting words from *Sharar*. This seems to be a sufficient reply to Botte's second additional point.

The most significant point indeed to emerge from a comparison of Section C with its counterpart in *Sharar* is the fact that both anaphoras contain the *Sanctus*, which creates a presumption in favour of its having belonged to the original common core. Sauget's edition gives only *incipit*s for the *Sanctus*, so that we are unable to make any comparison between the text of the *Sanctus* itself in the two anaphoras. In the introductory material the parallels are fairly close as far as the third word in l. 16, but thereafter the two texts diverge almost completely.

In l. 14 the verb ܣܓܕ ('adore') occurs at the beginning of the enumeration of heavenly beings in Addai and Mari and evidently applies to the whole list; in *Sharar* it follows ܟܠܗ, and thus applies only to the first group. It is then balanced by ܡܫܒܚܝܢ ('glorify') at the end of l. 15 with the myriads as the subject of this verb. The second clause, however, is nearly twice as long as the first, and the parallelism of *Sharar* is not obviously superior to that of Addai and Mari. The connection of ܡܫܒܚܝܢ with ܫܡܟ ('thy name') in the latter forms a link with l. 11 and may be felt to be more primitive. *Sharar*'s list of heavenly beings is shorter than that of Addai and Mari, although several of the additional words noted by Engberding (1932) are probably secondary within the textual tradition of Addai

and Mari (see textual notes on ll. 14–15). If we retain the word-order
of Addai and Mari and excise all words that are not attested in both
anaphoras (except for ܐܠܗܐ), we obtain the following text:

ܠܘܬ ܪܒܘܬܟ ܡܪܝ ܐܠܦ ܐܠܦܝܢ ܥܠܝ̈ܐ .ܪܒܒܝ̈ܬܐ

ܡ̈ܫܬܐ ܕܢܘܪܐ ܘܕܪܘܚܐ. ܡܫܒܚܝܢ ܠܫܡܟ ܥܡ ܟܪ̈ܘܒܐ ܘܣ̈ܪܦܐ.

Thy majesty, O my Lord, a thousand thousand heavenly beings and myriad
myriads of hosts, the ministers of fire and of spirit, adore, glorifying thy name
with the cherubim and the seraphim.

It seems probable that this is a close approximation to the original
common core of the two anaphoras at this point. Engberding remarks
on the brevity of the enumeration of heavenly beings, only the
thousands and myriads of Dan. 7: 10 being added to the cherubim
who normally accompany the seraphim of Isaiah, a restraint found
also, as he points out, in the Anaphora of Chrysostom (*LEW*, p. 322,
ll. 24–6). The word translated 'hosts' means literally 'encampments',
but is also used of the troops that occupy them. Here the thought is
clearly of the heavenly hosts, a usage that may be compared to that of
Gen. 32: 2–3 (1–2 in the English versions), where the same word is
used in the Peshitta. The phrase 'the ministers of fire and of spirit'
derives from Ps. 104: 4; the word 'spirit' might also of course be
translated 'wind'.

After the third word of l. 16 the anaphoras are very different in
their immediate introduction to the *Sanctus*, and Engberding declines
to make a judgement in favour of either form. There are, however,
two substantial points that favour the originality of Addai and Mari.
In the first place its l. 17 is in exact agreement with the Peshitta of Isa.
6: 3, whereas *Sharar* prefixes ܡܢ ('from', i.e. 'from one to another'),
suppresses ܩܪܐ ('calling'), and inserts several other verbs before
ܘܐܡܪܝܢ ('and saying'). These verbs include ܡܥܐ ('crying out'),
which is in l. 16 of Addai and Mari and thus probably belongs to the
common core. It is possible, however, that the last three words of
l. 16, which could well be a secondary expansion, did not belong to
the common core.

After ܘܐܡܪܝܢ ('and saying') *Sharar* inserts a petition: 'with whom,
O my Lord, by thy grace and mercies may we also be accounted
worthy to say three times'. Serapion has a similar petition at this
point, but in *Sharar* it does break the natural sequence from ܘܐܡܪܝܢ
('and saying') to ܩܕܝ ('Holy') very abruptly, and this suggests that it

is secondary here. At this point it is also necessary to take into account the difference between the two anaphoras at the beginning of Section D where, as we have seen, the first four words of l. 21 and the first word of l. 22 are absent from *Sharar*. Macomber pointed out the significance of the emphatic pronoun 'we' in *Sharar* (see above), but did not appear to notice that the probable reason for the absence of the connecting words from *Sharar* is that they have been replaced by the additional petition so awkwardly inserted between ll. 17 and 18. Both here and at the beginning of Section D *Sharar* seems to have the secondary text.

NOTES ON THE TRANSLATION

16 'ceaselessly': lit. 'without ceasing'. This is probably an allusion to Rev. 4:8.

17 'to one another': lit. 'this one to this one', which corresponds exactly to the Hebrew idiom.

D

In this section are to be found some of the closest parallels between the Anaphoras of Addai and Mari and *Sharar*, and we need not hesitate to reckon the material common to both as constituting a very ancient text. For practical purposes it will be convenient to divide this passage into three main subsections: ll. 21–3, 24–30, and 31–3. The Congregational *Amen* in l. 34 and the diaconal injunction to prayer in l. 35 require no comment.

The first subsection (ll. 21–3) introduces the congregation's thanksgiving for redemption, which may be regarded as the heart of the anaphora. Sufficient attention has already been given to the probable reason for the absence from *Sharar* of the first four words of l. 21 and the first word of l. 22. We may, however, draw attention to the fact that both Cyril (*Cat. Myst.* 5. 6 *ad fin.*) and Theodore (Mingana, pp. 100 and 239) emphasize the joining of the earthly congregation in the worship of the heavenly beings, Theodore actually using the words ܐܦ ܚܢܢ ('we also') as at the beginning of l. 22. We may also note the striking parallel in the introduction to the post-*Sanctus* in the Byzantine liturgy, especially in the Anaphora of Chrysostom (*LEW*, p. 324, ll. 5–7): μετὰ τούτων καὶ ἡμεῖς τῶν δυνάμεων . . . βοῶμεν καὶ λέγομεν, and the less verbally close parallel in the sixth-century fragment edited by Connolly (1925, p. 102, ll. 19–24).

The three self-deprecating adjectives attached to ܥܒ̈ܕܝܟ ('thy servants') at the end of l. 22 recur in a similar context in l. 51, where there is no parallel in *Sharar*; here *Sharar* has as their counterpart the single adjective ܚܛ̈ܝܐ ('sinful'). Spinks (1980) is probably right in suggesting that these words are a devotional phrase peculiar to the East Syrians, and it is probable that no self-deprecating adjectives at all were attached to ܥܒ̈ܕܝܟ in the common core of the anaphoras. In l. 23 the Anaphora of Addai and Mari again qualifies ܠܐܠܗܘܬܟ by ܪܡܬܐ as in l. 13, and here too it is to be regarded as a secondary accretion (see above, p. 84). With the excision of the last three words of l. 22 and the fourth word of l. 23 we obtain the common core of the two anaphoras. Engberding (1932) notes that ܡܘܕܝܢ in l. 21 exactly corresponds to εὐχαριστοῦμεν, and we may recall that this is how the anaphora in Hippolytus' *Apostolic Tradition* begins after the opening dialogue (see above, p. 82). We may also note that ܢܦܝܫܘܬܐ in l. 21 is used in much the same sense as ܬܫܒܘܚܬܐ in l. 15, and is perhaps chosen here as a more direct allusion to ܣܒܐܘܬ (*Sabaoth*) in the *Sanctus* itself.

The second subsection (ll. 24–30) celebrates the fact of redemption from the standpoint of human experience in a series of striking contrasts. The most important point to emerge from a comparison of the two anaphoras here is that that of Addai and Mari seems to have suffered a series of expansions in ll. 28–30 which obscure the structure and parallelism of the passage. There is no counterpart in *Sharar* to l. 30 at all, or to ܡܪܢ ܘܐܠܗܢ ('our Lord and God') in l. 28, while *Sharar*'s counterpart to the last three words of l. 29 is the single word ܒܨܝܪܘܬܢ ('our unworthiness'). *Sharar* clearly preserves the more primitive text at this point.

The remaining differences between the two anaphoras in this subsection are probably to be ascribed to the accidents of scribal transmission. They concern such matters as the conjunctions linking the several clauses, the presence or absence of the accusative particle *lamadh*, and the use of synonyms. The transposition in *Sharar* of the second half of l. 26 and the first half of l. 27 is probably to be similarly explained, there being no obvious superiority in either order of these clauses. In two instances where the anaphoras differ that of Addai and Mari seems to preserve the intrinsically superior reading: ܡܦܘܠܬܢ ('our fallen state') seems a more appropriate object for

ܐܘܩܝܡ ('raise up') than *Sharar*'s ܡܣܘܚܝ ('our casting out') in
l. 25 (although if Macomber, 1982, is right in translating the latter
'prostration' this objection would have less force), and ܚܝܘ is more
elegant than a repetition of the Aph'el of ܚܝܐ at the beginning of
l. 26 (where both words mean 'resurrect' or 'restore to life').

At all events the high degree of common matter here suggests that
this passage belongs to the oldest stratum of the anaphora, a
conclusion strengthened by the features noted by Engberding:
concentration on the central act of redemption by Christ, expressed
in a series of elevated contrasts. These are in themselves reminiscent
of the moving passage in *Pesahim* 10. 5 (Danby, p. 151):

Therefore are we bound to give thanks, to praise, to glorify, to honour, to
exalt, to extol, and to bless him who wrought all these wonders for our fathers
and for us. He brought us out from bondage to freedom, from sorrow to
gladness, and from mourning to a Festival-day, and from darkness to great
light, and from servitude to redemption; so let us say before him the *Hallelujah*.

Wegman (p. 35) appropriately draws attention to the *Paschal Homily*
of Melito of Sardis; one might note particularly ll. 473–6 and 760–4 in
the edition of Hall (1979). Other interesting parallels are in Hippolytus (p. 50, ll. 12–18) and the sixth-century fragment edited by
Connolly (1925, p. 112, ll. 14–20). None of these affords precise
parallels to our text, but they all indicate that it belongs to a definite
and early tradition with roots in Jewish forms.

We may also note a few echoes of biblical thought and language in
this subsection. The language of l. 24 recalls 2 Cor. 5: 19, John 5: 21,
and 2 Pet. 1: 4. The first half of l. 25 recalls 1 Sam. 2: 7. The root
meaning of ܚܘܒܐ in l. 26 is 'debt', while that of ܚܛܝܬܐ in l. 27 is
'to miss'. These distinctions are familiar from the Hebrew and Greek
biblical terms for 'sin'. The roots recur in ll. 57 f. where, however,
both the actual terms used denote concrete instances of sin so that we
have been able to differentiate in the translation between 'sins' and
'shortcomings'. The word rendered 'sinfulness' in l. 27 really describes
a state of continued shortcoming. The first word in l. 27, translated
'acquit', is the word 'justify' with all its biblical overtones. The second
half of l. 27 recalls Eph. 1: 18, and one wonders, in view of the
patristic use of φωτίζειν, whether there may not also here be an
allusion to Baptism.

The last subsection is the doxology in ll. 31–3, for which comparison must be made with the final doxology in ll. 60–6. Both doxologies

are introduced by the formula ܠܥܠ ܐܦ̈ܝ ('for'; literally 'in front of' and
hence 'for the sake of'/'on account of'), with which Engberding aptly
compares the anaphoras of Chrysostom (*LEW*, p. 322, l. 13) and
Apostolic Constitutions 8 (*LEW*, p. 18, l. 24). In l. 31 *Sharar* omits
ܛܒ̈ܬܐ ܘ ('benefits and') and reads a feminine suffix with ܟܠܗܝܢ
('all') which now qualifies ܛܝܒ̈ܘܬܟ ('graces') alone, and it is
probable that ܛܒ̈ܬܐ ܘ is an interpolation in Addai and Mari.
Engberding points out that it is a word for which the East Syrian
liturgies have a special predilection. It occurs in the sixth-century
fragment edited by Connolly (1925, p. 110, l. 19). On the other hand
Sharar's insertion of ܗܠܝܢ ('these') is also probably secondary. In l. 32
Sharar again inverts the order of the verb and the objects (as in l. 14),
and retains only the first two of the four nouns in Addai and Mari. In
view of what has been said above about the centrality of thanksgiving
in this part of the anaphora, it would be surprising if ܬܘܕܝܬܐ
('thanksgiving') were not original at this point, and ܣܓܕܬܐ ('adoration') also picks up a term which has been used in ll. 11 and 14. The
only one of the four nouns that has not been used previously is in fact
ܐܝܩܪܐ ('honour'), and this is securely attested in both texts. This
word is used to render כבוד ('glory'), e.g. in 1 Sam. 4: 21 f. and 1 Kgs.
8: 11, the word that occurs at the end of the *Sanctus* in Isa. 6: 3,
although as we have seen a different Syriac word is used to render it
in that passage. ܐܝܩܪܐ is nevertheless a highly appropriate doxological term to include in an anaphora.

For l. 33 *Sharar* has only the *incipit* ܘܗܫܐ ('now'), which prevents
any comparison of the texts of this line. Before this *incipit*, however,
Sharar inserts a line which it also reads at the corresponding point
before its equivalent of l. 66. This reads:

ܒܥܕܬܟ ܩܕܝܫܬܐ ܘܩܕܡ ܡܕܒܚܟ ܗܢܐ ܡܚܣܝܢܐ

in thy holy Church before thy propitiatory altar.

There is a very limited parallel to this in l. 62 of the Anaphora of
Addai and Mari, where the first word occurs, but in connection with
other material which *Sharar* attaches in a slightly different form to its
equivalent of l. 61. Macomber (1982) points out that there are
references elsewhere in the anaphora to the holy Church (l. 49) and
to the altar (l. 40), although ܡܚܣܝܢܐ ('propitiatory') does not occur
in Addai and Mari, and on this account he retains the line. It may,
however, be doubted whether it has any place in this first doxology,

since neither Church nor altar has yet been mentioned. It is simpler to believe that *Sharar* has assimilated the doxology here to its form of the final doxology. Engberding draws attention to the mention of the Church in the doxology of Hippolytus, and it probably derives ultimately from Eph. 3: 21.

NOTES ON THE TRANSLATION

23 'in a way' is a paraphrase necessitated by the substitution of an English idiom for the Syriac ܪܚܒܘܬܐ ܠܐ. Strictly 'which cannot be repaid' describes ܪܚܒܘܬܐ ('grace').

24 'assume': lit. 'clothe thyself with'. Spinks (1980) draws attention to Murray (1975, p. 311) for a useful summary of the Syriac use of this metaphor for the Incarnation. See the whole section (pp. 310–12). One may also compare Melito (Hall, ll. 309 and 452).

25 'our fallen state': literally 'our fall'. The meaning is: 'raise us up when we had fallen'.

26 'resurrect our mortality': i.e. 'raise us up when we were dead'.

31 'benefits': the root meaning of the word is 'aid', 'succour'.

E–F

It will be convenient to consider these two sections together since, despite the congregational *Amen* in l. 42, the grammatical structure shows that they form a continuous whole. The two sections jointly constitute the intercession. There are close parallels with *Sharar* in ll. 36–40 and 47b–50, although there is very little common matter in the intervening material in the two anaphoras.

At first sight l. 36 seems to make a new beginning after the doxology of ll. 31–4, and there is no immediately obvious connection with what has preceded. In both texts, however, if we ignore the intervening *Cushapha* in Addai and Mari, the common core underlying ll. 36–40 follows immediately after the doxology of ll. 31–4. The connection is heightened in *Sharar*, which contains the word ܡܛܠ ('therefore') between the second and third words of l. 36. Engberding (1932, p. 44), remarked on the parallel with *Te igitur* in the Gregorian Canon. The logical connection, however, does not appear to be the same. Willis (1964, pp. 123 f.), following Ratcliff, gives a clear indication of the probable sequence of thought in the Gregorian Canon: 'It is very meet . . . that we should give thanks to thee . . . we therefore humbly beseech thee . . . to accept and bless these gifts . . .

which we offer to thee . . . ' The word *igitur* indicates that the offering
of the elements is the sacrifice of praise and thanksgiving of which
God has been said to be worthy. In the common core of the
Anaphora of Addai and Mari and *Sharar* the most probable
sequence of thought is as expounded by Macomber (1982, p. 77):
'What is implied here would seem to be a prayer to God to associate
those who have died with the thanksgiving of angels and mortal men.
Behind the words of the prayer there seems to be a vision of a cosmic
act of praise and thanksgiving in which all creation shares—angels,
mortal men, and even those men who have died.' The word
'therefore' is hardly a natural link in this context, unless we connect it
specifically with the reference to the propitiatory altar at the end of
Section D which we saw to be peculiar to *Sharar*. In that case the
sequence of thought would be a plea that in view of the sacrifice of
praise offered at the propitiatory altar, God would remember for
good the souls of the departed, a thought very much on the lines of
that of Cyril of Jerusalem (*Cat. Myst.* 5. 8–10), which seems to reflect
a theology later and more explicit than that reflected in the
Anaphora of Addai and Mari. We conclude therefore that ܡܛܠ is a
secondary element in *Sharar*, and that Macomber's explanation of the
structure of the anaphora at this point is correct.

An examination of the parallel material in the two anaphoras in
ll. 36–40 makes it relatively easy to establish the original common
core simply by deleting material found in only one of the anaphoras.
The last two words of l. 36, the last word of l. 37, and the last two
words of l. 38 have no counterpart in *Sharar*, and are therefore to be
regarded as secondary accretions in Addai and Mari. The last of
these recurs in l. 59, where also it is without parallel in the
corresponding text of *Sharar*. In ll. 36–8, therefore, apart from its
insertion of ܡܛܠ *Sharar* preserves the core text. In l. 39 *Sharar*, in view
of its consistent address to Christ throughout the anaphora, lacks
ܕܡܫܝܚܟ ('of thy Christ') and reads second-masculine-singular
suffixes to 'body' and 'blood' ('in the commemoration of thy body
and blood'). In addition to the wider question of the address of the
anaphora as a whole it needs to be asked whether it is likely that the
memorial of Christ's body and blood would have been made directly
to him rather than to the Father in the original core text. In l. 40
Sharar reads a second-masculine-singular suffix with 'altar' (as do
some MSS of Addai and Mari), but this does not seriously affect the
sense. In place of the first adjective qualifying the altar (ܗܢܐ,

'pure') *Sharar* reads ܚܝܐ ('living'), which seems intrinsically less probable. *Sharar* throughout has a stronger interest in the altar than the Anaphora of Addai and Mari, in which this is its only mention. The last three words of l. 40 seem to have been amplified in *Sharar* by the additions of ܣܒܪܢ ('our expectation') and ܒܐܘܢܓܠܝܘܢ ܩܕܝܫܐ ('in thy holy Gospel'), to the second of which there is a parallel in l. 46 of Addai and Mari, to which we must return. It seems then that in ll. 39–40 it is the Anaphora of Addai and Mari rather than *Sharar* that has preserved the common-core text.

It is at this point that the texts of the two anaphoras diverge sharply from one another, and they do not really rejoin company until Section H. At first sight *Sharar* seems to preserve a more direct continuity at this point, but on closer examination its insertion of a paraphrase of John 6: 51 before the expected Institution Narrative belies this appearance. In addition to the curiosity of an Institution Narrative addressed to Christ we note again in the material following it the strongly propitiatory flavour reminiscent of Cyril's theology, which is foreign to the atmosphere of the Anaphora of Addai and Mari. The latter, on the other hand, introduces a new theme altogether in l. 41 in the form of an intercession for the living. There is first a prayer for peace in this world (l. 41), and then a prayer for the universal knowledge of God as revealed in Christ and in the religion he came to teach (ll. 43–50). It is in the latter part of this section (ll. 47b–50) that we find once again substantial parallels between the two anaphoras, although these are by no means simple to evaluate.

The parallel material consists in fact of the list of Christian leaders in ll. 47b–48, culminating in the mention of all baptized members of the Church in ll. 49–50. The four categories of leaders in l. 47b and the three orders of ministry in l. 48 are common to both lists, although *Sharar* has added a number of others. The first four words of l. 49 are common to both texts, as is the essential content of l. 50. *Sharar*'s participle ܪܫܝܡܝܢ ('signed') in place of the two words at the beginning of l. 50 may be felt to be simpler and more direct, but its adjective ܡܚܣܝܢܝܬܐ ('propitiatory' or 'absolving') in place of ܩܕܝܫܐ ('holy') describing baptism seems to reflect its own particular theological stance. In ll. 47b–50 then we conclude that the common-core text has been preserved in the Anaphora of Addai and Mari, except for its addition of the last word of l. 49 and its paraphrase at the beginning of l. 50.

What is interesting, though not yet entirely explicable, is that the common material in ll. 47b–50 occurs in quite different contexts in the two anaphoras. In *Sharar* it is clearly in the context of an offering of the Eucharist in memory of departed Christians, and it is introduced by a repetition of some of the language of ll. 37–8 ('remembrance of all the upright and just fathers'), which it must be said makes a very satisfactory link with the list. In the Anaphora of Addai and Mari the common material is also introduced by a resumption of language used in the earlier common-core passage. The clause 'and he taught us in his life-giving Gospel' picks up the end of l. 40, where we found a similar reference to the Gospel in *Sharar*. This is followed here by 'all the purity and holiness of', which leads directly into the list. In Addai and Mari the categories listed seem less sharply differentiated into the living and the departed, although it must be noted that after the common material *Sharar* itself goes on to offer intercessions for various categories of the living. The essential difference is that in *Sharar* the context of the list is the offering of the Eucharist in memory of departed Christians, while in Addai and Mari it is part of the commemoration of the revelation of true religion brought by Christ. What is curious is that the list is introduced in the two anaphoras by the resumption of material from the earlier common-core passage, but by different material in each case.

Engberding (157, pp. 107 f.), draws attention to the fact that the 'thou hast taught us' of l. 40 is picked up by 'he . . . taught us' in l. 46, and that the reference to the Gospel attached to it in l. 46 is found in the parallel to *Sharar* in l. 40. He then suggests that the phrase 'all the purity and holiness' in l. 47 is adapted from the description of the altar in l. 40 as 'pure and holy'. These close links between ll. 40 and 46 f. point, he thinks, to an original continuity of the two common-core passages in the two anaphoras, the intervening material in each case being a secondary insertion. Following Engberding's lead with a few minor modifications, we might thus restore a primitive continuous text:

ܐܢܬ ܡܪܝ، ܒܪ̈ܚܡܝܟ ܣ̈ܓܝܐܐ
ܥܒܕ ܕܘܟܪܢܐ ܛܒܐ ܠܟܠܗܘܢ ܐܒ̈ܗܬܐ ܟ̈ܐܢܐ ܘܙܕ̈ܝܩܐ.
ܒܥܘܗܕܢܐ ܕܦܓܪܗ ܘܕܡܗ ܕܡܫܝܚܟ.
ܕܩܪܒܝܢ ܠܟ ܥܠ ܡܕܒܚܐ ܕܟܝܐ ܘܩܕܝܫܐ
ܐܝܟܢܐ ܕܐܢܬ ܐܠܦܬܢ ܒܣܒܪܬܗ ܡܚܝܢܝܬܐ.

ܒܝ ܢܐܘܬܐ ܘܥܠܝܐ ܘܡܗܝܪܐ ܘܡܢܕܪ
ܘܐܒܗܘܬܐ ܕܟܐܢܐ ܘܕܙܕܝܩܐ.
ܘܠܟܠܢ ܬܘܕ ܢܝܫܐ ܕܒܛܝܒܘܬܟ.
ܢܨܝܪܢ ܒܪܘܫܡܐ ܕܡܥܡܘܕܝܬܐ ܩܕܝܫܬܐ.

Do thou, O my Lord, in thy manifold mercies
make a good remembrance for all the upright and just fathers
in the commemoration of the body and blood of thy Christ,
which we offer to thee upon the pure and holy altar,
as thou hast taught us in his life-giving Gospel:
the prophets and apostles and martyrs and confessors
and bishops and priests and deacons
and all the children of the holy Church
signed with the sign of the holy Baptism.

At first sight such a restoration removes the obscurities, accounts for the repetitions, and yields a clear and intelligible text which consists solely of the material common to the two anaphoras. There are, however, a number of obstacles in the way of accepting this as the complete original text of this part of the anaphora.

In the first place, even in this reconstruction there is an awkward distance separating the initial mention of the fathers in the second line from the detailed list of categories into which they fall in the last four lines, and we have already observed that in *Sharar* the substance of the second line is repeated before the list, yielding a more satisfactory sequence. If this reconstruction corresponded in substance to the primitive text, it would be much improved if the third, fourth, and fifth lines were transferred to the end.

In the second place, as Macomber (1971, p. 78) points out, the insertion of different matter into the supposed original prayer is supposed to have occurred in both anaphoras at the same point in the common core. This is certainly difficult to explain, and it seems more reasonable to suppose that the common-core material was already separated into two sections before the anaphoras went their separate ways. This suggests that Engberding's brilliant hypothesis, if well founded at all, relates to a rather earlier stage in the evolution of the common core than to that at which the two anaphoras were developed independently from one another.

A further point made by Macomber (1971, p. 77) is that Engberding's analysis leaves only the reconstruction of common-core material from Sections E and F between D and Section H, since he has shown that Section G is dependent on the first part of Section F, which he regards as secondary. This means that the anaphora as reconstructed by Engberding consists solely of the thanksgiving, a prayer for the departed, the *epiklēsis* and the final doxology, and that the only reference to the institution of the Eucharist would be that contained in the third, fourth, and fifth lines of the reconstruction of Sections E and F. To this point may be added the detail that there would seem to be little antecedent for ܡܒܪܢܘܬܟ ('thy dispensation') in l. 60, which is common to both anaphoras, if ll. 54–5 are deleted.

If we are right in thinking that the two common-core passages in ll. 36–40 and 47b–50, even if they once represented a continuous prayer, were already separated before *Sharar* and Addai and Mari went their separate ways, we have to consider afresh the possibility that the intervening material in ll. 41, 43–6 belonged here already at that time. We have given reasons above for regarding the intervening material in *Sharar* as stemming from a later period than that of Addai and Mari. We have also offered an analysis of the sequence of thought in Sections E and F of the Anaphora of Addai and Mari as they stand. It must certainly be admitted that this is much less logical and orderly than the structure of Sections A–D, and one possibility is that we have here a loose amalgam of short passages which were in the process of becoming traditional.

Engberding (1957, pp. 100–13) examines the material in ll. 41, 43–6 which is without parallel in *Sharar*. He notes a number of significant parallels, some of them exclusive, with the Anaphora of Theodore and comes to the conclusion that the reviser of Addai and Mari has abbreviated this material from Theodore and incorporated it. This conclusion has been effectively questioned, however, by Botte (1965, pp. 97 f.), who asks pertinently whether the reviser would have rearranged the logical order of the material as found in the Anaphora of Theodore, and in particular whether his abbreviation would have been likely to result in a more exact allusion to John 17: 3 in ll. 43–5. The evidence, he suggests, points rather to a dependence of Theodore on Addai and Mari. This biblical allusion, found also in Serapion (see below), may indeed be a mark of antiquity.

There are some suggestive parallels in the sixth-century fragment edited by Connolly (1925, p. 114). The section begins after a lacuna, and unfortunately much of this page of the fragment is missing, but at least part of Connolly's reconstruction is convincing, and the passage evidently consists of a series of intercessions. For our purposes three

specific points are of significance. The word 'peace' in l. 16 suggests
a parallel with l. 41 of our text. Lines 17–23 seem to be a prayer for
the several orders of ministers in the Church (note Connolly's
argument for the identification of the word 'priesthood' in l. 18),
corresponding to l. 48 of our text. In ll. 24–6 there is evidently a
prayer for the departed, including a clear mention of confessors and
the pair of adjectives 'upright and just' used in reference to the
fathers in l. 38 of our text. This clearly supports the connection
between ll. 37 f. and 47b of our text reflected in *Sharar*. The greatest
significance of this passage of the fragment, however, lies in the fact
that the categories in l. 47b of our text are separate from those in
l. 48, the former belonging clearly to the commemoration of the
departed and the latter to the intercessions for the living. It is also
significant that in the fragment the intercession for the departed
comes in the middle of that for the living (ll. 28 ff. appear to go on to
pray for kings). This material may therefore serve to strengthen the
hypothesis that Sections E and F of the Anaphora of Addai and
Mari represent an amalgam of traditional material which has been
put together in a not very orderly way, in which some of the
material is found here in a context different from that in which it
originated.

We may therefore make the tentative suggestion that l. 47b originally belonged at the end of l. 38, and that l. 47a originally
belonged to ll. 48–50 and was an intercession for the ministers and
other members of the Church. The last two words of l. 46 probably
belong to l. 40 as reflected in *Sharar*, and the remainder of l. 46 is
probably to be explained as a not very successful attempt to provide a
link between ll. 43–5 and 47–50 after the original order of the
material had been dislocated. If this analysis is correct, the original
text of Sections E and F will have comprised (a) an intercession for
the departed, (b) an intercession for the world, asking for peace and
for the universal knowledge of God in Christ, and (c) an intercession
for the ministers and other members of the Church. The broad
structure of this intercession has been preserved in the present text of
Addai and Mari, and, as we shall see, Section G follows on as a
natural sequel.

How does such an intercession compare with the oldest anaphoral
texts available to us? There is no parallel to any of the intercessory
material in Hippolytus. There are, however, some interesting parallels in Serapion. There is an allusion to John 17: 3 in the exordium of

the anaphora, and there is a brief and general intercession at the end, including a memorial of the departed. There are no direct verbal links between the two texts, but they may be felt to breathe the same atmosphere, and in particular to antedate the new propitiatory theology of intercession at the Eucharist propounded somewhat self-consciously by Cyril of Jerusalem.

One detail that emerges from the comparison with Serapion's *Euchologion* is the greater sophistication in the terminology for 'remembrance' and 'commemoration' in Addai and Mari. The *Euchologion* actually uses the term ἀνάμνησις for the memorial of the departed, and is perhaps free to do so because it does not use this term for the eucharistic memorial (its Institution Narratives does not include the command to 'Do this in remembrance of me'). It is interesting that while the Peshitta New Testament uses ܕܘܟܪܢܐ for ἀνάμνησις in the Institution Narratives (Luke 22: 19, 1 Cor. 11: 24 f.), as does the Old Syriac in the former passage, the Anaphora of Addai and Mari uses ܥܘܗܕܢܐ (l. 39), just as it later uses the cognate verb ܥܗܕ (l. 53) for the eucharistic commemoration, while it uses ܕܘܟܪܢܐ (l. 37) for the memorial of departed Christians. Ledogar (pp. 35 f.) draws attention to the use of ܥܗܕ of the eucharistic commemoration in 1 Cor. 11: 26, where it renders καταγγέλλετε, and suggests that it has overtones of 'proclamation' and especially 'praise'. He points out that in l. 53 the 'praise' verbs precede the 'commemoration'. This seems to indicate that the Anaphora of Addai and Mari makes a conscious distinction between the 'remembrance' of the departed and the eucharistic 'commemoration' of the body and blood of the Lord.

Finally we note the clear presence of both *anamnēsis* and oblation in ll. 39–40, even though they are mentioned only in a subordinate phrase and are not made the subject of a separate section or sections of the anaphora. The passage is not so very different from the corresponding passage attached directly to the Institution Narrative in Hippolytus' *Apostolic Tradition*, where it admittedly enjoys a greater prominence: 'Memores igitur mortis et resurrectionis eius, offerimus tibi panem et calicem, gratias tibi agentes . . .' We may also note the position of the oblation before the Institution Narrative in Serapion, and the fact that the eucharistic commemoration is made in that anaphora by linking the oblation to the Institution Narrative without the use of any specifically anamnetic language. In all three anaphoras we seem to witness the emergence of themes that are to become dominant at a period when there is still great fluidity in the structure of the Eucharistic Prayer.

It remains to draw attention to a few details. The 'good remembrance' of l. 37 is reminiscent of the prayer of Nehemiah: 'Remember me, O my God, for good' (Neh. 13: 31, cf. also 14 and 22). The preposition 'in' at the beginning of l. 39 may mean no more than that the Eucharist is the appropriate occasion for prayer for the departed. It may also suggest their participation in the eucharistic celebration, as was proposed by Macomber. What is not suggested is any pleading of the sacrifice of either the Cross or the Eucharist as a ground of the intercession for the departed (contrast Cyril of Jerusalem). The antecedent of 'which' at the beginning of l. 40 is not entirely clear. It could possibly be the 'body and blood of thy Christ', but this would imply a much more advanced theology of the eucharistic sacrifice than is otherwise present in this anaphora (the nearest parallel would be the use of the term 'offering' of the elements in l. 56). Much more probably the antecedent of 'which' is the 'commemoration', referring to the whole eucharistic action undertaken in fulfilment of the dominical command. The clause 'as thou hast taught us' in l. 40 is clearly addressed to God, but the specific reference is equally clearly to the institution of the Eucharist at the Last Supper and the dominical command to observe it. It is not unreasonable to regard God the Father as the ultimate source of this 'teaching', and if we are right in following *Sharar* in attaching the phrase 'in his life-giving Gospel' (l. 46) directly to this clause, any obscurity is dispelled. The 'teaching' of Christ in l. 46 of the present form of the text is reminiscent of Matt. 28: 20, while the mention of Baptism in l. 50 recalls the previous verse.

NOTES ON THE TRANSLATION

36 'and ineffable': lit. 'which cannot be told'.

37 'gracious': lit. 'acceptable' (see also p. 69 above).

41 'make with us': this is a literal translation; the sense is presumably 'establish for us' or 'grant to us'.   'peace': the word is cognate with Hebrew שלום (*shalom*), denoting 'welfare' in a wide sense.

47 'prophets': the position before 'apostles' suggests that the reference is to the Old Testament prophets rather than to Christian prophets.

48 'priests': literally 'elders' (cf. $\pi\rho\epsilon\sigma\beta\acute{v}\tau\epsilon\rho\sigma$).

50 'signed . . . sign': this is not the root used for 'seal' in the Peshiṭta of 2 Cor. 1: 22, Eph. 1: 13, 4: 30.

G

This paragraph is often regarded as the most problematical in the whole Anaphora of Addai and Mari. The problems it raises, however, may not appear completely insoluble. The first fact that confronts us is that this Section has no counterpart at all in *Sharar*. This has naturally led some to question its originality in the Anaphora of Addai and Mari. It certainly excludes the possibility of detecting secondary accretions to the text by the process of comparative analysis. There are, however, two phrases that may reasonably be suspected of being secondary accretions. The self-deprecating description of 'we . . . thy . . . servants' in the fifth, sixth, and seventh words of l. 51 has already occurred in l. 22, where we found reason to regard it as secondary. The last two words of l. 54 also have the appearance of a later reverential addition, breathing the atmosphere of Cyril of Jerusalem's 'awe-inspiring hour'. Ratcliff (1929) suggests the omission of these adjectives on the ground that they destroy the balance of the antithesis between 'example' and 'mystery'. Apart from these two phrases there appear to be no intrinsic grounds for questioning the originality of the detailed contents of this paragraph.

The chief difficulty is to determine the relationship of Section G to the rest of the anaphora. On this depends very largely its interpretation. We have already noted that l. 55 affords an appropriate antecedent to 'thy . . . dispensation' in l. 60, so much so that it has led some to suspect the originality of Section H on the ground that it breaks the continuity between Section G and Section I. The difficulty of connection lies rather at the beginning of Section G. It arises partly from grammatical obscurity, and partly from the question of the overall structure of the anaphora. It will be wise to begin with the grammatical questions.

In the first place it is clear that the 'we also' of l. 51 implies either addition or contrast to others who have been previously mentioned, and the determination of who these others may be is an important part of the problem of interpretation. The most serious grammatical problem however arises from the fact that the paragraph appears to lack a main verb, despite the attempts of exegetes to treat one or more of the verbs as a main verb. Macomber (1971, p. 70, n. 4) points out that the present participle in Syriac also serves on occasion as the present tense. He proposes to separate the participle at the beginning of l. 54 from the series of participles preceding it in l. 53. In the absence of any differentiation in the text, however, it seems preferable to treat these participles as a continuous series (each after the first being introduced by the copula *waw*), prefixed by the particle ܟܕ at the beginning of l. 53, which indicates that they continue the sense of the two participles at the end of l. 51 after the parenthetic clause in the past tense in l. 52. The whole series is thus governed by the *dalath* introducing the eighth word in l. 51, and is grammatically a series of relative clauses describing the 'we also' at the beginning of the paragraph. Macomber (1982, pp. 87, 88, n. 22) appears to recognize this grammatical structure. Renaudot (2. 586) arbitrarily treats the last two in the series of participles in ll. 53–4 as main verbs. Brightman (*LEW*, p. 287, l. 22) translates 'both stand before thee . . . and have received', but Botte (1949, p. 267) points out that this rests on an unsatisfactory treatment of the second of the two participles at the end of l. 51 and the perfect at the beginning of l. 52 as coordinate main verbs, connected with repeated *waw* which he renders 'both . . . and'. Botte's own suggestion that the perfect at the beginning of l. 52 is the main verb, the *waw* being merely adverbial, is a *tour de force*. All these attempts to find a main verb within Section G must be judged unsuccessful, and, unless textual corruption is presupposed, the verb of which 'we also' is subject must be understood as repeated from what precedes.

In the present form of the text only one verb in the previous paragraph appears to be a grammatically possible predicate for the 'we also' of l. 51, and that is the verb at the beginning of l. 43. The sense then is 'that all the inhabitants of the world may know thee . . . and we also', and it must be said at once that this is both grammatically and conceptually satisfactory. It does mean that the whole of ll. 41–55 constitutes a single, rather straggling, sentence, but this cannot be excluded on a-priori grounds.

It is possible, however, as we have seen, that the material in Sections E–F is not in its original form. Engberding (1957, pp. 114 f.) concludes that Section G is a continuation of what precedes, although he regards it as a secondary insertion. In his reconstruction, however, ll. 47b–50 are regarded as a continuation of the commemoration of the departed in ll. 36–40. He is able to cite several instances in other anaphoras in which a prayer for the living is attached to the prayer for the departed with the formula 'we also'. He correctly remarks that 'we also' fits well after the reference to all the baptized members of the Church in ll. 49–50, but his analogy of the *casus pendens* construction is justly criticized by Botte (1965, pp. 102 ff., cf. 1949, p. 267). He points out that the *dalath* that introduces all the categories enumerated in ll. 47b–50 would need to be repeated at the beginning of l. 51 if this were to be the grammatical sequel to what immediately precedes. In the reconstruction tentatively proposed in the previous part of this Commentary an even better connection becomes possible. Lines 48–50 were there regarded as an intercession for the ministers and other members of the Church, and what could be more natural than that a prayer for the present congregation should be attached to this with the formula 'And we also'? In this case the verb of which 'we' is the subject will be the same as that of which the categories enumerated in ll. 48–50 are the subject. In the Appendix we have suggested in the light of Connolly's reconstruction of the sixth-century fragment (Connolly, 1925, p. 114) that this verb is 'stand'. The sequence of thought is then: 'may they stand before thee in all purity and holiness, the bishops . . . and all the children of the holy church . . . and we also . . . who are gathered and stand before thee'. The repetition of the words 'stand before thee' will serve as a further link between the two sections. It may be objected that this reconstruction is hypothetical, but even if it is rejected, we have seen that a perfectly satisfactory grammatical sense may be obtained if the verb at the beginning of l. 43 is taken as the predicate also of the 'we' of l. 51. The grammatical problems then are seen to be soluble, and the identification of the others to whom 'we also' are added or contrasted will be all the inhabitants of the earth, if the present text is retained, the departed, if Engberding's reconstruction is followed, and the ministers and other members of the Church, if the reconstruction proposed above is accepted. In each case a satisfactory sense is obtained.

Before we go on to examine some other aspects of the place of Section G within the anaphora as a whole, we must take note of two quite different interpretations of this paragraph. In a series of articles Botte (1949, 1954*b*, 1965) put forward the hypothesis that l. 51 presupposes a now lost Institution Narrative which it immediately followed. This he thinks ended like the Narrative in the Anaphora of Theodore (Kelaita, p. 69): 'and thus be ye doing whenever ye are gathered for my memorial.' The immediate sequel to this in the Anaphora of Theodore has obvious parallels with our text: 'And as we have been commanded we also thy unworthy, frail and miserable servants have gathered that . . . we may celebrate this great and awesome mystery.' Botte's argument is that the word 'gathered' is a deliberate resumption of the 'whenever ye are gathered' of the now lost Institution Narrative, and that the 'we also' contrasts the present congregation with the original disciples at the Last Supper to whom the words were first thought to be addressed.

This interesting and suggestive hypothesis is certainly worthy of serious consideration. An ultimate evaluation of its probability will depend to a considerable extent on the conclusion reached on the question whether the anaphora ever did contain an Institution Narrative, the wider aspects of which have already been considered in the introduction to this Commentary. Here it must be stated that the greatest weakness in Botte's exegesis of Section G, which he treats together with what he regards as its continuation in Section I as an *anamnēsis*, is his failure to establish a main verb so that the paragraph can stand satisfactorily on its own. We must also note that Botte's additional suggestion that the phrase 'gathered in thy name' may reflect an Institution Narrative such as that contained in a sermon of Ephraim, which included the clause: 'And when you are gathered in my name' (Botte, 1949, pp. 273 f.), founders on the fact that the word ܒܫܡܟ ('in thy name') is missing from l. 51 in the two oldest MSS, which of course were not available when Botte wrote. Botte's more general points about the anamnetic character of the contents of Section G will be considered below.

Raes (1970) follows a different line of interpretation altogether. If Section G's closest parallel in the Anaphora of Theodore is the *anamnēsis* following the Institution Narrative, its closest parallel in the Anaphora of Nestorius follows the intercessions and precedes the *epiklēsis*, i.e. its position is exactly analogous to that of Section G in the Anaphora of Addai and Mari. What is different is that the prayer in the Anaphora of Nestorius leads directly into the *epiklēsis* with its main verb: 'We . . . thy unworthy, frail and miserable servants . . . whom . . . thou hast made worthy to stand before thee . . . supplicate thy . . . Godhead . . . and let the grace of the Holy Spirit come, O my Lord . . . ' (for Syriac text see Kelaita, pp. 98 f.). In the light of this parallel Raes suggests that in the Anaphora of Addai and Mari too Section G is the prayer of introduction to the *epiklēsis*. The chief weakness of this hypothesis is that Raes has to assume that the main verb(s) 'we pray God . . . we beg him' have fallen out of the text in all extant MSS. Another weakness, which Raes himself points out, is the absence of such a prayer introducing the *epiklēsis* in *Sharar*, although the *epiklēsis* itself seems to belong to the common-core text of the two anaphoras. As in the case of Botte's hypothesis, it must ultimately stand or fall by the criterion of whether it offers a satisfactory account of the grammar as well as of the sense of the passage.

The fact that neither Botte's nor Raes's hypothesis offers a satisfactory grammatical exegesis of the passage without resort to hypothetical emendation of the text must count in favour of the simpler view that Section G is structurally an appendix to the intercessions of Sections E–F. If we accept this view, however precisely we conceive the connection between the three sections, we need to consider the significance within the anaphora as a whole of the material in Section G. Its similarity to ll. 39–40 is immediately obvious, and it may be suggested that the function of both passages is to set the intercessory material in the context of the celebration of the Eucharist, once near its beginning and once at its end.

The last three words of l. 51 state the context in general terms: this is an assembly of Christians who perform their priestly function of 'standing before' God to minister to him in divine service. The last two words are an echo of Deut. 10: 8, an expression also found in the *anamnēsis* of Hippolytus: 'Memores igitur mortis et resurrectionis eius, offerimus tibi panem et calicem, gratias tibi agentes quia nos dignos habuisti adstare coram te et tibi ministrare.' The root ܪܟܢ ('assemble, gather') is cognate with the root used in Hebrew to denote the synagogue, and the clear implication is that the present congregation has assembled for a synaxis. The nature of this synaxis and the priestly service offered at it is further defined in l. 52 by what is clearly a reference to the institution of the Eucharist at the Last Supper. Spinks (1980) draws attention to the verb ܩܒܠ ('receive'), which corresponds to the technical rabbinic term for 'receiving' tradition, a Greek equivalent of which is used also by St Paul when introducing his Institution Narrative in 1 Cor. 11: 23. The word ܡܫܠܡܢܘ ('tradition') denotes the succession of oral tradition to which the Institution Narrative belongs, and the word ܛܘܦܣܐ (τύπος, 'example'), which in itself means a 'type' or 'likeness', in this context clearly implies that what the Lord said and did at the Last Supper was a pattern that the Christian congregation is intended to follow. The second-masculine-singular suffix in ܡܢܟ ('from thee') can be explained in the same way as 'thou hast taught us' in l. 40.

Having clearly defined the nature of the Eucharistic assembly, the anaphora goes on in l. 53 to express the particular functions of praise and proclamation that constitute the heart of the eucharistic celebration. The series of participles reaches its climax in ܚܕܒܢ in l. 54. The ordinary meaning of the verb ܥܒܕ is 'to do' or 'to make', and Spinks (1980) appropriately renders it 'perform'. Its Hebrew cognate עבד, however, is also used on occasion in the special sense of offering sacrifice, e.g. in Isa. 19: 21. With this usage in mind, we have ventured to render it here by the word 'celebrate', which has acquired similar overtones as a word regularly used for carrying out the eucharistic liturgy. The word ܐܪܙܐ ('mystery') can also denote a type, symbol, figure, or likeness, but it is the natural word for a sacrament and the term 'mystery' with its overtones in New Testament and patristic Greek of the saving acts of God, once concealed in his hidden purpose, but now revealed in historical reality, and realized afresh in the present in both cultic representation and spiritual experience, seems an appropriate rendering. This term is also used in the sixth-century fragment edited by Connolly (1925, p. 112): 'he took bread and wine . . . made it holy with a spiritual blessing. And he left this awesome mystery to us.' Here the saving acts are summed up very succinctly in l. 55 as the passion, death, and resurrection of Christ. Only the last two are mentioned at this point in Hippolytus, although the passion has been mentioned earlier in the anaphora. All three are found in *Apostolic Constitutions* 8 (*LEW*, p. 20, ll. 28–9), although the Ascension and *parousia* are added there. Serapion has no parallel to this material.

Putting together the contents of ll. 39–40 and Section G we observe that the Anaphora of Addai and Mari contains the following elements:

(a) statements that this is a eucharistic gathering for priestly service (l. 51) and offering (l. 40) and cultic celebration (l. 54);

(b) an *anamnēsis* of the passion, death, and resurrection of Christ (ll. 53–5) or variously of his body and blood (l. 39); and

(c) a deliberate reference of the present celebration to the institution of the Eucharist at the Last Supper (ll. 40b and 52).

There may be no formal Institution Narrative and no independent *anamnēsis* as a separate section of the anaphora, but it cannot be denied that the substance of both such elements is clearly present in the anaphora in such a way as to suggest that it is of primary importance in determining the nature of what is being done. Botte (1954*b*, p. 19), in his examination of the *anamnēsis* of Hippolytus draws attention to three elements: a recollection of the Institution, the enumeration of the saving mysteries, and a prayer of offering. All three elements are present in the Anaphora of Addai and Mari. The distinctive feature is that they are mentioned indirectly in the course of setting the intercessions within the context of the eucharistic celebration, and that they are not put together to form an *anamnēsis* as a distinct section within the anaphora.

H

With this section we return to the part of the text where a common core underlies both the Anaphora of Addai and Mari and *Sharar*, and where a comparative analysis makes possible a reasonably probable reconstruction of this common core. In its parallel to l. 56 *Sharar* has two additions (ܚܝܐ ܘ, 'living and' and ܘܥܡܪ, 'and dwell'), both of which are found also in some MSS of Addai and Mari, but are probably secondary accretions. The first two words of l. 57 are absent from *Sharar*, and may also be suspect on the grounds that they reflect a concept of 'consecration' of the elements suggesting a period later than that of the rest of the anaphora. *Sharar* reads *waw* in place of *dalath* before ܢܗܘܐ ('and let it be' rather than 'that it may be'), which is probably to be rejected as the result of a textual corruption (*dalath* and *waw* being easily confused in the process of copying) since it breaks the logical sequence of the prayer. *Sharar* also reads ܠܡܩܒܠܢܘܗܝ ('to those who receive it') in place of ܠܢ ('to us'), which seems to reflect adaptation to circumstances in which there is no longer a general communion of the whole congregation. On the other hand, the ܡܪܝ ('O my Lord') in l. 57, which has no counterpart in *Sharar*, seems to be an unnecessary duplication of that in the previous line. The first two and the fifth words of l. 57 are therefore probably not part of the original common core, while the third and fourth words seem to have been preserved more accurately in the Anaphora of Addai and Mari than in *Sharar*. In l. 58 the substance of the third and fourth words is absent from *Sharar*, the *waw* and *lamadh* being attached directly to the fifth word in place of *dalath* (omitting 'the great hope of'), and this shorter text of *Sharar* is probably original here. On the other hand, *Sharar*'s adjective ܒܪܝܟܬܐ ('blessed') attached to 'resurrection' is also likely to be secondary.

The last four words of l. 59 are absent from *Sharar*, which has simply ܠܥܠܡܝܢ ('for ever', literally 'to the ages') in their place. In this connection, compare the absence of the last two words of l. 38 from the parallel in *Sharar*. This seems to be another East Syrian traditional expression which has been added to the original context, and both it and *Sharar*'s simpler alternative are to be rejected as secondary. The *epiklēsis* which emerges as the common-core text can easily be seen in the Appendix.

The presence of such an *epiklēsis* in the common core underlying the two anaphoras proves, as Macomber (1982) points out, that it must have been present in the anaphora at any rate before the separation of the Churches after the Council of Ephesus in 431. This does not, however, preclude the possibility, which Macomber himself accepts, that the *epiklēsis* does not belong to the original text of the anaphora. He thinks that it was inserted during the fourth century, perhaps in reaction to Arian attacks against the divinity of the Holy Spirit. Against this must be set the evidence of Basil that the *epiklēsis* was an ancient tradition (see the Introduction, Section B). We have already mentioned the argument that Section H is secondary because it interrupts the sequence between Sections G and I. This was put forcibly by Botte (1954*b*, p. 19 and 1965, p. 101). He is undoubtedly correct in seeing in the reference to the saving acts of Christ in l. 55 the antecedent of ܡܕܒܪܢܘܬܟ ('thy dispensation') in l. 60, but the text he uses contains the reading with the demonstrative adjective in place of the suffix ('this dispensation'), which we have considered to be secondary (see the textual note on l. 60[1°]). The fact that *Sharar* has the reading with the suffix ('thy dispensation') strengthens the probability that this was the original reading, the adjective 'this' belonging to the secondary reading. This in turn weakens Botte's argument for an immediate sequence from l. 55 to l. 60. The additional argument in Macomber (1982, p. 81) that the original function of the *epiklēsis* has already been fulfilled, depends on his adoption of the *anamnēsis* of *Sharar* as part of the original text.

Botte (1965, pp. 99 f.) allows the possibility that the *epiklēsis*, though not original in its present context, may have been displaced from an earlier different position in the anaphora. He draws attention to its Semitic parallelism, and suggests that it derives at least from the same milieu as the rest of the anaphora. A comparison with other early forms of the *epiklēsis* will help in the assessment of the antiquity of the common core of the *epiklēsis* underlying *Sharar* and the

Anaphora of Addai and Mari. Before we turn to such a comparison, however, it must be noted that in both these anaphoras the *epiklēsis* immediately precedes the final doxology, and there is no evidence for its ever having occupied a different position. The reference in l. 60 at the beginning of the final doxology to the 'dispensation' of the saving acts looks back over the prayer as a whole, and does not require that l. 55 should have immediately preceded. The case for the *epiklēsis* having been interpolated at this point has not been made out.

There is a striking similarity between the common core of the *epiklēsis* in *Sharar* and the Anaphora of Addai and Mari and the oldest extant text of the *epiklēsis*, that of Hippolytus: 'Et petimus ut mittas Spiritum tuum sanctum in oblationem sanctae ecclesiae: in unum congregans des omnibus qui percipiunt sanctis in repletionem Spiritus sancti ad confirmationem fidei in veritate, ut te laudemus et glorificemus . . .' The combination of an invocation of the Holy Spirit on the offering, i.e. presumably the eucharistic elements, with a prayer for the fruits of communion and the absence of any prayer for a change in the elements are exclusive to these anaphoras and to the Maronite Anaphora of Xystus quoted by Botte (1954*a*) and Eng-berding (1957). This last is presumably related to *Sharar* rather than directly to the Anaphora of Addai and Mari and will not be discussed further here.

It is also worthwhile comparing the common core of the *epiklēsis* of the two Syrian anaphoras with the earliest form of that in the Anaphora of Basil (E-Basil, i.e. the shorter form, found only in a MS from Egypt) as published by Fenwick (pp. 18–22):

ἐλθεῖν τὸ πνεῦμα σου τὸ ἅγιον ἐφ᾽ ἡμᾶς καὶ ἐπὶ τὰ προκείμενα δῶρα ταῦτα καὶ ἁγιάσαι καὶ ἀναδεῖξαι ἅγια ἁγίων. καταξίωσον ἡμᾶς μεταλαβεῖν τῶν ἁγίων σου εἰς ἁγιασμὸν ψυχῆς καὶ σώματος ἵνα γενώμεθα ἓν σῶμα καὶ ἓν πνεῦμα καὶ εὕρωμεν μέρος μετὰ πάντων τῶν ἁγίων τῶν ἀπ᾽ αἰῶνος εὐαρεστησάντων σοί.

The most striking common element is the use of the verb 'come' rather than 'send' (as even in Hippolytus). On the significance of this verb, not least for the antiquity of this form of *epiklēsis*, see Spinks (1976, pp. 25 f.). Without accepting the whole of his argument it is interesting to observe that he dates the *epiklēsis* of the Anaphora of Addai and Mari as earlier than that of Basil. In the light of this it is also interesting to note parallels in Basil's *epiklēsis* with two elements that our comparison with *Sharar* has suggested do not belong to the

common core of the two Syrian anaphoras: the second word of l. 57
and the last four words of l. 59. Is it possible that the text of Basil's
epiklēsis has influenced the later development of that in the Anaphora
of Addai and Mari?

The later forms of the *epiklēsis* in the Anaphora of Basil (see
Fenwick, pp. 18–22) reflect a much more specifically consecratory
understanding of its purpose, with a specific petition for the 'consecration' of the elements of bread and wine as the Body and Blood of
Christ. This understanding is certainly reflected in Cyril, *Cat. Myst.* 5.
7, and is found already in the highly distinctive *epiklēsis* of the Logos
in Serapion. The absence of this element from the common core of the
epiklēsis in the two Syrian anaphoras suggests a date for it earlier than
the mid-fourth century, and thus militates against Macomber's
suggestion that it was inserted as a reaction against Arian attacks on
the divinity of the Holy Spirit.

A final comparison may be made with a passage in Ephrem
Syrus' Hymn 20 *de Juliano Saba* (CSCO 322 (Syr. 140), p. 74, stanza
4), cited by Atchley (1935, pp. 56, 58):

> ܥܠ ܗܘ ܚܝܐ ܕܣܡܐ ܢܚܬ ܪܘܚܐ
> .ܩܕܝܫܐ ܗܘ ܗܡܢ ܬܡܢ ܢܣܒ ܕ ܣܒܐ ܬܒܪ.

The Holy Spirit descended there
upon that medicine of life which Saba broke.

Although there are no verbal links between this passage and the
common-core *epiklēsis* of the two Syrian anaphoras, this is clearly a
reference to a eucharistic *epiklēsis*. Whether or not the traditional
ascription of the hymns on Julian Saba to Ephrem is correct, there is
no reason to question the historicity of the reference to Julian Saba's
celebration of the Eucharist. Since, according to the Edessene
Chronicle, he died in 367 (Murray, p. 92), we have here clear
evidence for the *epiklēsis* in Osrhoene in the mid-fourth century.
Similar, though less explicit, allusions are to be found in Ephrem's
Hymn 10 *de Fide*, stanzas 8 and 12.

The results of these comparisons suggest that the common core of
the *epiklēsis* of the two Syrian anaphoras is certainly earlier than the
mid-fourth century, and the fact that its closest affinity is to that of
Hippolytus suggests that it may well date back to the third century.
While it is possible that the *epiklēsis*, though early, was a relatively late
element in the earliest evolution of the anaphora, in the absence of

textual evidence this must remain a pure hypothesis. What does emerge from our study is that there is nothing in either the content or the position of the common core of the *epiklēsis* of the two Syrian anaphoras that is inconsistent with its belonging to the original anaphora.

NOTES ON THE TEXT

56 ᕽᕽᕽᕽᕽ ('And let . . . come'): Spinks (1976, p. 26) draws attention to the variant in the Lord's Prayer at Luke 11: 2: 'may thy Holy Spirit come (ἐλθέτω) upon us and cleanse us', which he suggests may be connected with the *epiklēsis*. ᕽᕽᕽᕽ ('and rest'): Spinks (1980) points out that this verb is derived from Isa. 11: 2, as is the additional verb ᕽᕽᕽ ('dwell') found in *Sharar* and in some MSS of the Anaphora of Addai and Mari. ᕽᕽᕽ ('offering'): the context makes it plain that the reference here is to the elements, but the language is very similar to that of Hippolytus (*oblationem*).

57b–58a Cf. the notes on 26–7 in Section D, p. 92.

58b–59a Observe the strong eschatological note, and cf. Serapion's use of the phrase 'medicine of life' as in the hymn of Ephrem Syrus cited above, which probably derives ultimately from Ignatius' similar phrase 'medicine of immortality' (Eph. 20. 2).

NOTE ON THE TRANSLATION

58 'from the dead': lit. 'from the house of the dead'.

I

This section comprises the final doxology, and invites comparison with the first doxology in ll. 31–4 of Section D. The structure and contents of ll. 31 and 60 are similar, the one important difference being the replacement of the ᕽᕽᕽᕽ ('all thy graces') of l. 31 with ᕽᕽᕽᕽ ('thy dispensation') as the common core of the two anaphoras in l. 60. Each anaphora has additional matter peculiar to itself: that of Addai and Mari prefaces the core word with ᕽᕽ ('all') and follows it with ᕽᕽᕽ ('wonderful'), while *Sharar* simply follows it with ᕽᕽᕽ ('glorious'), which is a variant found in two MSS of Addai and Mari. All this additional matter is probably secondary. The word ᕽᕽᕽᕽ is used to render the Greek οἰκονομία, particularly in its technical sense in relation to Christ's

incarnate life and redeeming work. As such it is a specially appropriate term to use here with reference back to the enumeration of the
passion, death, and resurrection of Christ in l. 55. This reference
is more explicit in *Sharar*, where the suffix ('thy') unambiguously
denotes Christ. In Addai and Mari, however, the term may well be
used in its more inclusive sense of the divine providence and purpose,
although still with special reference to the redemptive acts of the
incarnate Christ as suggested by the context. For this reason it is
rendered in our translation by the wider term 'dispensation'. The
variant reading without the suffix in many MSS of Addai and Mari
does not materially affect the meaning.

Lines 61 and 64 correspond broadly to l. 32. In l. 32 the simple ܩܡܒ
ܠܟ ('we offer thee') is followed directly by the four objects as in l. 64.
In l. 61 the doxology is expressed by two finite verbs ܐܘܚ
ܠܟ ܘܡܫܒܚ ('we give thee thanks and glorify thee'), to which the
participle ܕ ܡܩܪܒܝܢ ('offering') is then attached at the beginning of
l. 64 to introduce the four nouns. The last two words of l. 61, which
have no counterpart in *Sharar*, are probably secondary here as in l. 16,
to which perhaps they consciously refer: the earthly congregation
offers ceaseless praise like the heavenly choirs. If we delete this phrase,
which is probably inspired by Rev. 4: 8 (though not verbally
identical), the remainder of ll. 61 and 64 represent an amplified
version of l. 32. At that point, it will be remembered, *Sharar* contains
only the first two of the nouns and inverts the order of the verb and
object. Here, however, *Sharar* has an even shorter parallel, simply
ܡܘܕܝܢ ܠܟ ('we give thee thanks'), to which it attaches the further
description of the subject 'we': ܣܝ ܚܛܝܐ ܥܒܕܝܟ ('we thy sinful
servants'), yielding an almost exact equivalent of *Sharar*'s parallel to
ll. 21–2, the only difference being the omission here of the divine
address ܡܪܝ ('O my Lord'). Both here and in l. 32 it may be felt that
Sharar represents a reduced emphasis on praise and thanksgiving,
which the whole structure of the doxology suggests is primary to it as
to the anaphora as a whole.

Lines 62–3 have no counterpart in the earlier doxology of Addai
and Mari. The material in l. 62 is paralleled in two separate phrases
in *Sharar*. The first word ('in thy Church') is followed by four
additional words and comes immediately before the equivalent of
l. 66. This is in exact agreement with *Sharar*'s reading before l. 33 (see
above under Section D). Although both Church and altar have now
been mentioned, it is significant that the parallel in the doxology of

Hippolytus is confined to the simple 'in sancta ecclesia tua', and the reference to the propitiatory altar seems to be a characteristic addition of *Sharar*. The single word ܒܥܕܬܟ ('in thy Church') in the Anaphora of Addai and Mari corresponds to Eph. 3: 21, where it also occurs in a doxological context, and probably represents the original common core. *Sharar*'s parallel to the rest of l. 62 is attached to the phrase 'we thy sinful servants' instead of to 'thy Church'. The participle is in the masculine construct plural, and the suffix to 'blood' is in the second rather than the third person, the word ܕܡܫܝܚܟ ('of thy Christ') being omitted altogether in accordance with the consistent address to Christ in *Sharar*. The other difference is that the adjective describing the blood of Christ is not ܝܩܝܪܐ ('precious'), as in Addai and Mari, but ܙܟܝܐ ('innocent'). The whole phrase in *Sharar* therefore reads: ܦܪܝܩܝܢ ܒܕܡܟ ܙܟܝܐ ('redeemed by thine innocent blood'). It seems probable that there is an allusion here to 1 Pet. 1: 18–19, and when both texts are compared with the biblical passage it is clear that that of Addai and Mari is verbally closer to it, particularly in respect of the adjective 'precious'. The major difference between the two anaphoras at this point, however, is the context in which the adjectival phrase occurs. There is no direct biblical precedent for the description of the Church as redeemed by the blood of Christ, but it is possible that behind the text of Addai and Mari there lies a conflation of 1 Pet. 1: 18–19 with Acts 20: 28, and that the adjectival phrase has been detached from this context in *Sharar* to form a slightly awkward sequel to 'we thy sinful servants' in order to leave the ground free for *Sharar*'s additional reference to the propitiatory altar after the mention of the Church. If this is so, Addai and Mari will be judged to preserve the common core in its primitive form.

The first two words of l. 63 are found in *Sharar*, though in the (presumably collective) singular, and there is probably, as Spinks (1980) suggests, an allusion to Ps. 51: 17. He also suggests that the last two words, which have no counterpart in *Sharar*, are an allusion to 2 Cor. 3: 18. One might venture the further suggestion that there is here an intentional contrast with the seraphim of Isa. 6: 2 who cover their faces before the glory of God. The parallelism here may also favour the originality of Addai and Mari. At this point *Sharar* makes a slightly awkward link with its phrase beginning 'in thy Church' by repeating the verb 'give thanks' in the form of a singular participle attached to 'mouth', the whole phrase thus reading: 'with open mouth which gives thee thanks in thy holy Church . . .'. The need to make this connection may have been a reason for the absence from *Sharar* of the last two words of l. 63. The overall impression resulting from a comparison of ll. 62–3 with the parallel material in *Sharar* is that the text of Addai and Mari is more primitive in both order and content, and that *Sharar* shows signs of rearrangement of some of the material.

There is no counterpart at all in *Sharar* to l. 65, but, as Macomber (1982) points out, the mention of 'thy name' may well be a reference back to ll. 11 and 15. Three adjectives may perhaps be felt to reflect some degree of expansion, and one might have expected ܚܝܐ ܘܡܚܝܢܐ ('living and life-giving') to be adjacent. This might suggest that ܩܕܝܫܐ ('holy') is secondary, but in itself it is more likely to be primitive with its echoes of the Lord's Prayer and the Jewish *Kaddish*.

Lines 66–7 are identical with ll. 33–4 and require no further comment. *Sharar* again has only the *incipit* ܡܟܝܠ ('now'), which precludes any further comparison of the two anaphoras at this point.

APPENDIX: A RECONSTRUCTION OF AN EARLIER FORM

I T may be worthwhile attempting the restoration of an earlier form of the Anaphora of Addai and Mari than can be reached on the basis of textual criticism alone in our present state of knowledge. The restoration attempted here is based solely on the literary-critical judgements made in the Commentary, and its hypothetical nature must be stressed. It may, however, be useful in facilitating ready comparison with reconstructions proposed by other scholars.

A

P ܠܡܫܝܚܘܬܗ ܕܡܪܢ ܢܣܒ ܡܫܝܚܐ. ܘܫܡܗ ܕܐܠܗܐ ܐܒܐ.
ܘܫܘܬܦܘܬܐ ܕܪܘܚܐ ܕܩܘܕܫܐ. ܬܗܘܐ ܥܡ ܟܠܢ.

R ܐܡܝܢ.
P ܠܥܠ ܡܕ̈ܥܝܟܘܢ.
R ܠܘܬܟ ܡܪܝܐ.
P ܢܘܕܐ ܠܡܪܝܐ.
R ܫܘܐ ܘܙܕܩ.

B

P ܫܘܐ ܠܫܘܒܚܐ ܡܢ ܟܠ ܦܘ̈ܡܝܢ. ܘܬܘܕܝܬܐ ܡܢ ܟܠ ܠܫ̈ܢܝܢ.

ܫܡܗ ܣܓܝܕܐ ܘܡܫܒܚܐ ܕܐܒܐ ܘܒܪܐ ܘܪܘܚܐ ܕܩܘܕܫܐ.

ܕܒܪܐ ܥܠܡܐ ܒܛܝܒܘܬܗ. ܘܥܡܘܪ̈ܘܗܝ، ܒܡܪܚܡܢܘܬܗ.

ܘܦܪܩ ܒܢ̈ܝܢܫܐ ܒܚܢܢܗ. ܘܥܒܕ ܛܝܒܘܬܐ ܠܘܬ ܡ̈ܝܘܬܐ.

C

ܠܪܒܘܬܟ ܡܪܝ، ܣܓܕܝܢ ܐܠܦ ܐ̈ܠܦܝܢ ܕܥ̈ܠܝܐ ܘܪܒܘ ܪ̈ܒܘܢ ܕܡܫܪ̈ܝܬܐ.

ܡܫܡ̈ܫܢܐ ܕܢܘܪܐ ܘܕܪܘܚܐ. ܠܫܡܟ ܡܫܒܚܝܢ ܥܡ ܟܪ̈ܘܒܐ ܘܣܪ̈ܦܐ.

ܟܕ ܩܥܝܢ ܘܩܪܝܢ ܗܢܐ ܠܗܢܐ ܘܐܡܪܝܢ.
R ܩܕܝܫ ܩܕܝܫ ܩܕܝܫ ܡܪܝܐ ܚܝܠܬܢܐ. ܕܡܠܝܢ ܫܡܝܐ ܘܐܪܥܐ ܡܢ
ܬܫܒܘܚܬܗ.

D

P ܘܥܡ ܗܠܝܢ ܚ̈ܝܠܘܬܐ ܫܡ̈ܝܢܝܐ ܡܘܕܝܢ ܠܟ ܡܪܝ، ܐܦ ܚܢܢ ܥܒ̈ܕܝܟ.

ܕܥܒܕܬ ܒܢ ܛܝܒܘܬܐ ܕܠܐ ܡܬܦܪܥܐ.

ܕܠܒܫܬ ܐܢܫܘܬܢ ܕܬܚܝܢ ܒܐܠܗܘܬܟ.

ܘܪܝܡܬ ܡܘܟܟܢ. ܘܐܩܝܡܬ ܡܦܘܠܬܢ.

A

Priest	The grace of our Lord Jesus Christ and the love of God the Father
	and the fellowship of the Holy Spirit be with us all.
Response	Amen.
Priest	Lift up your hearts [lit. 'Up with your hearts'].
Response	To thee, O Lord.
Priest	Let us give thanks to the Lord.
Response	It is meet and right.

B

Priest Worthy of praise from every mouth and thanksgiving from every tongue
is the adorable and glorious name of the Father and the Son and the Holy Spirit,
who created the world in his grace and its inhabitants in his loving-kindness,
and redeemed the sons of men in his mercy, and dealt graciously with mortals.

C

Thy majesty, O my Lord, a thousand thousand heavenly beings and myriad myriads of hosts,
the ministers of fire and of spirit, adore, glorifying thy name with the cherubim and the seraphim,
crying out and calling to one another and saying:

Response Holy, holy, holy is the Lord Almighty: the heavens and the earth are full of his glory.

D

Priest And with these heavenly hosts we give thee thanks, O my Lord, we also thy servants,
because thou hast dealt graciously with us in a way which cannot be repaid,
in that thou didst assume our humanity that thou mightest restore us to life by thy divinity,
and didst exalt our low estate, and raise up our fallen state,

ܘܣܓܕܬ ܡܫܝܚܘܬܟ. ܘܫܒܚܬ ܣܘܟܠܟ.
ܘܙܕܩܬ ܠܫܠܝܘܬܟ. ܘܐܬܗܪܬ ܠܡܪܕܟ.

ܘܣܓܕܬ ܠܬ̈ܟܠܕܒܝܢ. ܘܚܙܝܬ ܠܚܝܪܘܬܟ.

ܘܟܠ ܐ̈ܦܝ ܟܠܗܝܢ ܠܦܬܘܬܝ ܕܠܘܬܟ.

ܢܣܩ ܠܟ ܬܫܒܘܚܬܐ ܘܐܝܩܪܐ ܘܬܘܕܝܬܐ ܘܣܓܕܬܐ.
ܗܫܐ ܘܒܟܠܙܒܢ ܘܠܥܠܡ ܥܠܡܝܢ.
R ܐܡܝܢ.

E–F

P ܐܢܬ ܡܪܝ ܒܪ̈ܚܡܝܟ ܦ̈ܓܥܐ
ܥܒܕ ܕܘܟܪܢܐ ܛܒܐ ܠܟܠܗܘܢ ܐܒ̈ܗܬܐ ܟ̈ܗܢܐ ܘܙܕܝ̈ܩܐ.

ܢܒ̈ܝܐ ܘܫ̈ܠܝܚܐ ܘܣ̈ܗܕܐ ܘܡܘ̈ܕܝܢܐ.
ܒܥܘܗܕܢܐ ܕܦܓܪܗ ܘܕܡܗ ܕܡܫܝܚܟ.
ܕܡܩܪܒܝܢ ܠܟ ܥܠ ܡܕܒܚܐ ܕܚܝܐ ܘܩܕܝܫܐ.
ܐܝܟܢܐ ܕܐܢܬ ܐܠܦܬܢ ܒܡܒܪܬܗ ܡܫܝܚܝܬܐ.
ܘܥܒܕ ܥܡܢ ܫܝܢܟ ܘܫܠܡܟ ܟܠܗܘܢ ܝܘ̈ܡܬܗ ܕܥܠܡܐ.

ܕܢܕܥܘܢ ܟܠܗܘܢ ܥܡ̈ܘܪܝܗ ܕܐܪܥܐ.
ܕܐܢܬ ܐܢܬ ܐܠܗܐ ܐܒܐ ܕܫܪܪܐ ܒܠܚܘܕܝܟ.
ܘܐܢܬ ܫܕܪܬ ܠܡܪܢ ܝܫܘܥ ܡܫܝܚܐ. ܒܪܟ ܘܚܒܝܒܟ.

ܘܗܘܝܘ ܡܪܚܡܢ ܒܟܠܗ ܕܚܝܘܬܐ ܘܩܕܝܫܘܬܐ
ܐܦܝܣܩܘܦܐ ܘܩܫܝܫܐ ܘܡܫܡ̈ܫܢܐ.
ܘܟܠܗܘܢ ܒ̈ܢܝܗ ܕܥܕܬܐ ܩܕܝܫܬܐ.
ܕܪܫܝܡܝܢ ܒܪܘܫܡܐ ܕܡܥܡܘܕܝܬܐ ܩܕܝܫܬܐ.

G

ܘܐܦ ܚܢܢ ܡܪܝ ܥܒ̈ܕܝܟ. ܕܟܢܝܫܝܢ ܘܩܝܡܝܢ ܩܕܡܝܟ.

ܘܡܩܒܠܝܢ ܒܝܘܒܠܐ ܛܘܦܣܐ ܕܡܢܟ.

ܟܕ ܚܕܝܢ ܘܡܫܒܚܝܢ ܘܡܪܡܪܡܝܢ ܘܡܥܗܕܝܢ.
ܘܥܒܕܝܢ ܠܗ ܠܐܪܙܐ ܗܢܐ
ܕܚܫܗ ܘܕܡܘܬܗ ܘܩܝܡܬܗ ܕܡܪܢ ܝܫܘܥ ܡܫܝܚܐ.

and resurrect our mortality, and forgive our sins,
and acquit our sinfulness, and enlighten our understanding,
and overcome our adversaries, and give victory to our
unworthiness.
And for all thy graces towards us
we offer thee glory and honour and thanksgiving and
adoration
now and at all times and for ever and ever.

Response   Amen.

E–F

Priest   Do thou, O my Lord, in thy manifold mercies
make a good remembrance for all the upright and just
fathers,
the prophets and apostles and martyrs and confessors,
in the commemoration of the body and blood of thy Christ,
which we offer to thee upon the pure and holy altar,
as thou hast taught us in his life-giving Gospel.
And make with us thy tranquillity and thy peace all the
days of the age,
that all the inhabitants of the world may know thee,
that thou alone art God the true Father,
and thou didst send our Lord Jesus Christ thy Son and thy
Beloved.
And may they stand before thee in all purity and holiness,
the bishops and priests and deacons
and all the children of the holy Church,
signed with the sign of holy Baptism.

G

And we also, O my Lord, thy servants, who are gathered
and stand before thee,
and have received by tradition the example which is from
thee,
rejoicing and glorifying and exalting and commemorating
and celebrating this mystery
of the passion and death and resurrection of our Lord Jesus
Christ.

H

ܘܬܐܬܐ ܡܪܝ ܪܘܚܟ ܩܕܝܫܐ ܘܬܬܢܝܚ ܥܠ ܩܘܪܒܢܐ ܗܢܐ ܕܥܒ̈ܕܝܟ.

ܕܢܗܘܐ ܠܢ ܠܚܘܣܝܐ ܕܚܘ̈ܒܐ. ܘܠܫܘܒܩܢܐ ܕܚܛ̈ܗܐ.

ܘܠܩܝܡܬܐ ܕܡܢ ܒܝܬ ܡ̈ܝܬܐ. ܘܠܚ̈ܝܐ ܚܕ̈ܬܐ ܒܡܠܟܘܬܐ ܕܫܡܝܐ.

I

ܘܥܠ ܟܠܗ̇ ܡܕܒܪܢܘܬܟ ܕܠܘܬܢ. ܢܘܕܐ ܠܟ ܘܢܫܒܚܟ.

ܒܥܕܬܟ ܦܪܝܩܬܐ ܒܕܡܗ ܝܩܝܪܐ ܕܡܫܝܚܟ.

ܒܦܘܡܐ ܦܬܝܚܐ ܘܒܐܦ̈ܐ ܓܠܝܬܐ.

ܟܕ ܡܩܪܒܝܢ ܬܫܒܘܚܬܐ ܘܐܝܩܪܐ ܘܬܘܕܝܬܐ ܘܣܓܕܬܐ ܠܫܡܟ
ܩܕܝܫܐ.

ܗܫܐ ܘܒܟܠܙܒܢ ܘܠܥܠܡ ܥܠܡܝܢ.

R ܐܡܝܢ.

NOTE

Only two elements in this reconstruction are not directly attested either in the MSS of the Anaphora of Addai and Mari or in the critical text of *Sharar* published by Sauget. In the opening dialogue the second response and the last exhortation are taken from the citations in Theodore of Mopsuestia's *Mystagogical Lecture* 16 (see the Commentary on Section A). The beginning of the eleventh line of Sections E–F: ܘܢܩܘܡܘܢ ܩܕܡܝܟ ܒ ('And may they stand before thee in') is derived from Connolly's reconstruction of the sixth-century fragment (Connolly, 1925, p. 114, l. 20) based on the Anaphora of Theodore. A similar passage occurs in Hippolytus, and is ultimately biblical (Deut. 10: 8; 18: 7). Note also the link with the first line of Section G. For details see the Commentary on Sections E–F and G.

H

And let thy Holy Spirit come, O my Lord, and rest upon
this offering of thy servants,
that it may be to us for the pardon of sins and for the
forgiveness of shortcomings,
and for the resurrection from the dead, and for new life in
the kingdom of heaven.

I

And for thy dispensation which is towards us we give thee
thanks and glorify thee
in thy Church redeemed by the precious blood of thy
Christ,
with open mouths and unveiled faces
offering glory and honour and thanksgiving and adoration
to thy holy name,
now and at all times and for ever and ever.

Response   Amen.

BIBLIOGRAPHY

TEXTS

Apostolic Constitutions, Books 7–8 in SC 336; Anaphora in Book 8 in *LEW*, pp. 3–27.

ASSEMANI, J. S., *Bibliotheca Orientalis Clementino-Vaticana* (Rome, 1719–28).

BASIL, *De Spiritu Sancto*, ed. B. Pruche (SC 17, 1947).

BRIGHTMAN, F. E., *Liturgies Eastern and Western, i.Eastern Liturgies* (Oxford, 1896, repr. 1965) = *LEW*.

CHABOT, J.-B., *Synodicon orientale, ou Recueil de synodes nestoriens* (Paris, 1902).

CHADWICK, H., *see* Origen.

CONNOLLY, R. H., *The Liturgical Homilies of Narsai* (Texts and Studies 8. 1, Cambridge, 1909).

—— 'Sixth-Century Fragments of an East-Syrian Anaphora', *OC* NS, 12–14 (1925), 99–128.

CUMING, G. J., *see* Hippolytus.

DANBY, H., *The Mishnah* (Oxford, 1933, repr. 1958).

DIX, G., *see* Hippolytus.

EPHREM, Hymn 10 *de Fide: St Ephrem, A Hymn on the Eucharist*, ed. and transl. Sebastian Brock (Hymns of Faith, No. 10, Lancaster, 1986).

HALL, S. G., *Melito of Sardis, On Pascha and Fragments* (Oxford Early Christian Texts, Oxford, 1979).

HIPPOLYTUS, *Apostolic Tradition*: text: ed. B. Botte (SC 11*bis*, 1968); translations: G. Dix, *The Apostolic Tradition*, reissued with additional material and corrections (London, 1968); G. J. Cuming, *Hippolytus: A Text for Students* (Grove Liturgical Study No. 8, Bramcote, 1976).

JASPER, R. C. D., and CUMING, G. J., *Prayers of the Eucharist: Early and Reformed*, 3rd edn. (New York, 1987) = *PEER*.

JUSTIN MARTYR, *see* Williams.

KELAITA, J. E. Y. DE, *The Liturgy of the Church of the East* (Mosul, 1928).

Liturgia Sanctorum Apostolorum Adaei et Maris (Urmia, 1890).

MINGANA, A., *Commentary of Theodore of Mopsuestia on the Lord's Prayer and on the Sacraments of Baptism and the Eucharist* (Woodbrooke Studies 6, Cambridge, 1933).

ORIGEN, *Dialogue with Heracleides*: text: J. Scherer, *Entretien d'Origène avec Héraclide et les évêques ses collègues* (Publications de la Société Fouad I de

Papyrologie 9, Cairo 1949); id., *Entretien d'Origène avec Héraclide* (SC 67, 1960); translation: H. Chadwick, 'Dialogue with Heracleides', *Alexandrian Christianity* (Library of Christian Classics 2, London, 1954), 430–55.

PHILLIPS, G., and HOWARD, G. *The Teaching of Addai*, transl. G. Howard (Syriac text repr. from G. Phillips, *The Doctrine of Addai* (London, 1876); Society of Biblical Literature Texts and Translations 16, Ann Arbor, 1981).

SAUGET, J. M., *Anaphora Syriaca Sancti Petri Apostoli tertia* (Anaphorae Syriacae 2. 3, Rome, 1973), 273–329.

SCHERER, *see* Origen.

SERAPION, *Euchologion*: text: F. E. Brightman, 'The Sacramentary of Serapion of Thmuis', *JTS* 1 (1900), 88–113; translation: J. Wordsworth, *Bishop Sarapion's Prayer-Book*, 2nd edn. (London, 1923).

SPINKS, B. D., *Addai and Mari—The Anaphora of the Apostles: A Text for Students* (Grove Liturgical Study No. 24, Bramcote, 1980).

Webb Archive: A collection of transcripts, photocopies, and microfilms of Syriac liturgical texts made by the late Revd Douglas Webb, now in the possession of St Gregory's House Library, Oxford.

WILLIAMS, A. LUKYN, *Justin Martyr, The Dialogue with Trypho*, transl. A. Lukyn Williams, with Introduction and Notes (London, 1930).

MODERN AUTHORS

AMAND DE MENDIETA, E. (1965), *The 'Unwritten' and 'Secret' APOSTOLIC TRADITIONS in the Theological Thought of St. Basil of Caesarea* (Scottish Journal of Theology Occasional Papers, No. 13, Edinburgh–London).

ATCHLEY, E. G. C. F. (1935), *On the Epiclesis of the Eucharistic Liturgy and in the Consecration of the Font* (Alcuin Club Collections, No. 31, Oxford).

BAUMSTARK, A. (1904), 'Altlibanesische Liturgie', *OC* 4: 190–4.

——(1923), 'Trishagion und Qeduscha', *JLW* 3: 18–32.

BOTTE, B. (1949), 'L'Anaphore chaldéenne des Apôtres', *OCP* 15: 259–76.

——(1954a), 'L'Épiclèse dans les liturgies syriennes orientales', *SE* 6: 48–72.

——(1954b), 'Problèmes de l'Anamnèse', *JEH* 5: 16–24.

——(1965), 'Problèmes de l'anaphore syrienne des Apôtres Addaï et Mari', *OS* 10: 89–106.

BOULEY, A., (1981), *From Freedom to Formula* (The Catholic University of America Studies in Christian Antiquity, No. 21, Washington, DC).

BOUMAN C. A. (1950), 'Variants in the Introduction to the Eucharistic Prayer', *VC* 4: 94–115.

BOUYER, L. (1968), *Eucharist*, transl. C. U. Quinn, (Notre Dame–London).

BRADSHAW, P. F. (1987), 'The Search for the Origins of Christian Liturgy: Some Methodological Reflections', *SL* 17: 26–34.

BRIGHTMAN, F. E. (1930), 'The Anaphora of Theodore', *JTS* 31: 160–4.

CAPELLE, B. (1951), 'L'Entretien d'Origène avec Héraclide', *JEH* 2: 143–57.

——(1952), 'Origène et l'oblation à faire au Père par le Fils, d'après le papyrus de Toura', *RHE* 47: 163–71.

CUMING, G. J. (1975), 'Pseudonymity and Authenticity, with Special Reference to the Liturgy of St. John Chrysostom', *SP* 15 (1984), 532–8.

——(1980), 'Thmuis Revisited: Another Look at the Prayers of Bishop Sarapion', *TS* 41: 568–75.

——(1981), *He gave thanks: an introduction to the Eucharistic Prayer* (Grove Liturgical Study, No. 28, Bramcote).

——(1984), 'Forum: Four Very Early Anaphoras', *Worship* 58: 168–72.

CUTRONE, E. J. (1973), 'The Anaphora of the Apostles: Implications of the Mar Eša'ya Text', *TS* 34: 624–42.

——(1978), 'Cyril's Mystagogical Catacheses and the Evolution of the Jerusalem Anaphora', *OCP* 44: 52–64.

DIX, G. (1945), *The Shape of the Liturgy*, 2nd edn. (London; repr. 1964).

ENGBERDING, H. (1929), 'Der Gruss des Priesters zu Beginn der εὐχαριστία in östlichen Liturgien', *JLW* 9: 138–43.

——(1932), 'Urgestalt, Eigenart und Entwickelung eines altantiochenischen eucharistischen Hochgebetes', *OC* 7 (29): 32–48.

——(1935), 'Nachhall altchristlicher liturgischer Akklamationen in den Šᵉlāvāthā der ostsyrischen Liturgie' in *Studien zur Geschichte und Kultur des Nahen und Fernen Ostens: Paul Kahle zum 60. Geburtstag*, ed. W. Heffening and W. Kirfel (Leiden), 47–54.

——(1957), 'Zum anaphorischen Fürbittgebet der ostsyrischen Liturgie der Apostel Addaj und Mar(j)', *OC* 41: 102–24.

FENWICK, J. (1986), *Fourth Century Anaphoral Construction Techniques* (Grove Liturgical Study, No. 45, Bramcote).

FIENSY, D. A. (1985), *Prayers Alleged to be Jewish: An Examination of the Constitutiones Apostolorum* (Brown Judaic Studies 65, California).

FINKELSTEIN, L. (1928–9), 'The Birkat ha-Mazon', *JQR* 19: 211–62.

FLUSSER, D. (1963), 'Sanktus und Gloria' in *Abraham unser Vater*: Festschrift für Otto Michel, ed. O. Betz, M. Hengel, and P. Schmidt (Leiden), 129–52.

FORTESCUE, A. (1912), *The Mass* (London).

GALVIN, R. J. (1973), 'Addai and Mari Revisited: The State of the Question', *EL* 87: 383–414.

GELSTON, A. (1982), 'ΔΓ ΕΥΧΗΣ ΛΟΓΟΥ (Justin, *Apology* i. 66. 2)', *JTS* NS 33: 172–5.

——(1991), 'Sacrifice in the Early East Syrian Eucharistic Tradition' in *Sacrifice and Redemption*, ed. S. W. Sykes (Cambridge), pp. 118–125.

GIRAUDO, C. (1981), *La struttura letteraria della preghiera eucaristica* (Analecta Biblica 92, Rome).

HANSON, R. P. C. (1961), 'The Liberty of the Bishop to Improvise Prayer in the Eucharist', *VC* 15: 173–6.

HEINEMANN, J. (1962), 'Birkath Ha-Zimmun and Ḥavurah-Meals', *JJS* 13: 23–9.

——(1977), *Prayer in the Talmud* (Eng. version by R. S. Sarason, Berlin).

JAMMO, S. Y. H. (1966), 'Gabriel Qaṭraya et son commentaire sur la liturgie chaldéenne', *OCP* 32: 39–52.

——(1979), *La Structure de la messe chaldéenne du début jusqu'à l'anaphore* (*OCA* 207, Rome).

JONES, BAYARD H. (1964*a*), 'The History of the Nestorian Liturgies', *ATR* 46: 155–76.

——(1964*b*), 'The Sources of the Nestorian Liturgy', *ATR* 46: 414–25.

——(1966), 'The Formation of the Nestorian Liturgy', *ATR* 48: 276– 306.

KILMARTIN, E. J. (1974), 'Sacrificium Laudis: Content and Function of Early Eucharistic Prayers', *TS* 35: 268–87.

LAMPE, G. W. H. (1961) (ed.), *A Patristic Greek Lexicon* (Oxford; repr. 1978).

LANE, D. J. (1981), 'Pervenimus Edessam: The Origins of a Great Christian Centre outside the Familiar Mediaeval World', *Florilegium* 3: *Carleton University Annual Papers on Classical Antiquity and the Middle Ages*, 104–17.

LEDOGAR, R. J. (1968), *Acknowledgement: Praise-Verbs in the Early Greek Anaphora* (Rome).

LIETZMANN, H. (1933), 'Die Liturgie des Theodor von Mopsuestia', *Sitzungsberichte der Preussischen Akademie der Wissenschaften* 23: 915–36 (repr. TU 74 (1962), 71–97).

——(1979), *Mass and Lord's Supper*, with the Introduction and Further Inquiry by R. D. Richardson (Leiden).

LIGIER, L. (1973), 'The Origins of the Eucharistic Prayer: From the Last Supper to the Eucharist', *SL* 9: 161–85.

MACOMBER, W. F. (1966), 'The Oldest Known Text of the Anaphora of the Apostles Addai and Mari', *OCP* 32: 335–71.

——(1971), 'The Maronite and Chaldean Versions of the Anaphora of the Apostles', *OCP* 37: 55–84.

——(1973), 'A Theory on the Origins of the Syrian, Maronite and Chaldean Rites', *OCP* 39: 235–42.

——(1975–6), 'An Anaphora Prayer Composed by Theodore of Mopsuestia', *PdO* 6–7: 341–7.

——(1977*a*), 'A History of the Chaldean Mass', *Worship* 51: 107–20.

——(1977*b*), 'The Sources for a Study of the Chaldean Mass', *Worship* 51: 523–36.

——(1982), 'The Ancient Form of the *Anaphora of the Apostles*' in *East of Byzantium: Syria and Armenia in the Formative period*, ed. N. G. Garsoïan, T. F. Mathews, and R. W. Thomson (Dumbarton Oaks, Washington), 73–88.

MAGNE, J. (1987), 'L'Anaphore nestorienne dite d'Addée et Mari et l'anaphore maronite dite de Pierre III: Étude comparative', *OCP* 53: 107–58.

MANNOORAMPARAMPIL, T. (1984), *The Anaphora and the Post-Anaphora of the Syro-Malabar Qurbana* (Kottayam).

MARSTON, W. (1989), 'A Solution to the Enigma of "Addai and Mari"', *EL* 103: 79–91.

MOUSSESS, C. (1951), 'Les Huit Éditions du missel chaldéen', *P-OC* 1: 209–20.

——(1952), 'La Liturgie chaldéenne des Apôtres', *P-OC* 2: 125–41.

——(1954), 'Les Missels chaldéens d'après les manuscrits, *P-OC* 4: 26–32.

MURRAY, R. (1975), *Symbols of Church and Kingdom* (Cambridge).

PRICE, C. P. (1961), 'Jewish Morning Prayers and Early Christian Anaphoras', *ATR* 43: 153–68.

RAES, A. (1944), 'Le Récit de l'institution eucharistique dans l'anaphore chaldéene et malabare des Apôtres', *OCP* 10: 216–26.

——(1970), 'The Enigma of the Chaldean and Malabar Anaphora of the Apostles' in *The Malabar Church*, ed. J. Vellian (*OCA* 186, Rome), 1–8.

RAHMANI I. E. (1899) (ed.), *Testamentum Domini Nostri Jesu Christi* (Mainz; repr. Hildesheim, 1968).

——(1929), *Les Liturgies orientales et occidentales* (Beirut).

RATCLIFF, E. C. (1929), 'The Original Form of the Anaphora of Addai and Mari: A Suggestion', *JTS* 30: 23–32 = *Liturgical Studies* (London, 1976), 80–90.

——(1963), 'A Note on the Anaphoras Described in the Liturgical Homilies of Narsai' in *Biblical and Patristic Studies in Memory of Robert Pierce Casey*, ed. J. N. Birdsall and R. W. Thomson (Freiburg-im-Breisgau), 235–49 = *Liturgical Studies*, 66–79.

REIF, S. C. (1983), 'Jewish Liturgical Research: Past, Present and Future', *JJS* 34: 161–70.

RENAUDOT, E. (1847), *Liturgiarum Orientalium Collectio*, 2 vols. (Frankfurt and London; republ. Farnborough, 1970).

SÁNCHEZ CARO, J. M. (1977), 'La anáfora de Addai y Mari y la anáfora maronita Šarrar: Intento de reconstrucción de la fuente primitiva común', *OCP* 43: 41–69.

SEGAL, J. B. (1970), *Edessa: 'The Blessed City'* (Oxford).

SPINKS, B. D. (1976), 'The Consecratory Epiklesis in the Anaphora of St. James', *SL* 11: 19–38.

——(1977), 'The Original Form of the Anaphora of the Apostles: A Suggestion in the Light of Maronite Sharar', *EL* 91: 146–61.

——(1980a), 'The Jewish Sources for the Sanctus', *Heythrop Journal* 21: 168–79.

——(1980b), 'A Note on the Anaphora Outlined in Narsai's Homily xxxii', *JTS* ns 31: 82–93.

——(1982–3), 'Priesthood and Offering in the Kuššāpê of the East Syrian

Anaphoras', *SL* 15: 104–17 = *LMD* 154 (1983), 107–26.

——(1984*a*), 'Addai and Mari and the Institution Narrative: The Tantalizing Evidence of Gabriel Qatraya', *EL* 98: 60–7.

——(1984*b*), 'Eucharistic Offering in the East Syrian Anaphoras', *OCP* 50: 347–71.

——(1985), 'Beware the Liturgical Horses! An English Interjection on Anaphoral Evolution', *Worship* 59: 211–19.

STEVENSON, K. (1980), '"Anaphoral Offering": Some Observations on Eastern Eucharistic Prayers', *EL* 94: 209–28.

——(1986), *Eucharist and Offering* (New York).

TALLEY, T. J. (1976), 'From Berakah to Eucharistia: A Reopening Question', *Worship* 50: 115–37.

VAN UNNIK, W. C. (1951), 'I Clement 34 and the "Sanctus"', *VC* 5: 204–48.

VELLIAN, J. (1972), 'The Anaphoral Structure of Addai and Mari', *Le Muséon* 85: 201–23.

VERHEUL, A. (1980), 'La Prière eucharistique de Addaï et de Mari', *QL* 61: 19–27.

WEBB, D. (1967–8), 'Variations dans les versions manuscrites de la liturgie nestorienne d'Addai et de Mari', *SE* 18: 478–523.

——(1970), 'La Liturgie nestorienne des Apôtres Addaï et Mari dans la tradition manuscrite' in B. Botte *et al.*, *Eucharisties d'Orient et d'Occident* (Lex Orandi 47, Paris), 25–49.

——(1980), 'An Introductory Note to the Manuscripts', in B. D. Spinks's edn. of *The Anaphora of the Apostles* (see Texts), pp. 30–2 (Webb also contributed readings of twelve MSS to Spinks's edn.).

——(1990), 'The Anaphora of Theodore the Interpreter', *EL* 104: 3–22.

WEGMAN, H. A. J. (1979), 'Pleidooi voor een tekst de anaphora van de Apostelen Addai en Mari', *Bijdragen* 40: 15–43.

WILLIS, G. G. (1964), *Essays in Early Roman Liturgy* (Alcuin Club Collections, No. 46, London).

Details of a few works not listed here are given where they are mentioned in the text.

INDEX OF BIBLICAL REFERENCES

INDEX OF REFERENCES
TO OTHER ANCIENT SOURCES

INDEX OF REFERENCES
TO MODERN AUTHORS